8/12

D0990143

you can RENEW this item from
home by visiting our Website at
www.woodbridge.lioninc.org or by
calling (203) 389-3433

**A Yankee Horseman
in the Shenandoah Valley**

A Yankee Horseman
in the Shenandoah Valley

The Civil War Letters of John H. Black,
Twelfth Pennsylvania Cavalry

Edited by David J. Coles and Stephen D. Engle

Voices of the Civil War
Peter S. Carmichael, Series Editor

The University of Tennessee Press / Knoxville

The Voices of the Civil War series makes available a variety of primary source materials that illuminate issues on the battlefield, the homefront, and the western front, as well as other aspects of this historic era. The series contextualizes the personal accounts within the framework of the latest scholarship and expands established knowledge by offering new perspectives, new materials, and new voices.

Photographs reproduced from the *Magazine of the Jefferson County Historical Society* (Charles Town, West Virginia), vol. 55 (December 1989).

The paper in this book meets the requirements of American National Standards Institute / National Information Standards Organization specification Z39.48-1992 (Permanence of Paper). It contains 30 percent post-consumer waste and is certified by the Forest Stewardship Council.

Library of Congress Cataloging-in-Publication Data

Black, John H., 1834–1922.
A Yankee horseman in the Shenandoah Valley: the Civil War letters of John H. Black, Twelfth Pennsylvania Cavalry / edited by David J. Coles and Stephen D. Engle.
     pages cm. — (Voices of the Civil War)
Includes bibliographical references and index.
ISBN 13: 978-1-57233-848-7 (hardcover)
ISBN 10: 1-57233-848-2 (hardcover)
  1. Black, John H., 1834–1922—Correspondence.
  2. United States. Army. Pennsylvania Cavalry Regiment, 12th (1861–1865)
  3. Pennsylvania—History—Civil War, 1861–1865—Personal narratives.
  4. United States—History—Civil War, 1861–1865—Personal narratives.
  5. Shenandoah River Valley (Va. and W. Va.)—History—Civil War, 1861-1865.
  I. Coles, David J.
  II. Engle, Stephen Douglas.
  III. Title.

E527.612th .B55 2012
973.7'8—dc23
2012017308

For James A. and Jayne P. Coles
and Taylor and Claire Engle

Contents

Illustrations

Preface

In many respects, John Henry Black was typical of the thousands of volunteers who fought for the Union during the Civil War. The son of Jacob and Mary Black, he had been born on his father's farm near Canan Station, Allegheny Township, Pennsylvania, on July 28, 1834. Black's grandfather, Adam, a native of Maryland, had been an early settler to the region and had operated a sawmill and grist mill in addition to serving as justice of the peace. Jacob Black was born about 1804 and raised in Greenfield Township, but following his marriage he moved to Allegheny Township, where he raised a family of nine children and farmed. In 1850 he owned real estate worth $4,500.00, and by 1860 the value had risen to $12,000.00, with a personal estate of $1,500.00.[1]

Blair County, in the south-central part of the state, had been formed in 1846 from Huntingdon and Bedford Counties. Its main towns were Altoona, Hollidaysburg, and Duncansville. Branches of the Juniata River cut through the county, as did parts of the Pennsylvania Canal and the Pennsylvania Railroad. More than thirty ironworks operated there by the 1850s, and lead, zinc, and coal were abundant. Despite the topography, which was somewhat mountainous, farming was not uncommon, with corn being the principal crop.[2]

John Black lived with his parents until the age of twenty, helping his father with farm chores and finding the time to obtain an education. He attended local schools and the Tuscarawas Academy in nearby Juniata County. About 1854 John began teaching in the public schools of Duncansville, Blair County, remaining in that profession until his enlistment at the outbreak of the war in the Fourteenth Pennsylvania Volunteer Infantry. At the time of the 1860 federal census, Black was living in Newry, Blair County, in the household of a merchant named James McIntosh.[3]

As Black grew to manhood, growing sectional disputes threatened the United States. The election of Abraham Lincoln in 1860 resulted eventually in the secession of eleven Southern states and the outbreak of civil war. Black's home state of Pennsylvania provided nearly 360,000 white soldiers for the Union cause, in addition to some 8,600 black recruits and thousands more men who served in the U.S. Navy. More than 33,000 were killed or mortally wounded during the war. Units from Pennsylvania, the second most populous state in the Union, comprised a significant percentage of the total number of Union servicemen, particularly in the Eastern theater of the war. A number of prominent generals, including George Meade, George McClellan, John Reynolds, and Winfield Scott Hancock, also hailed from the Keystone State. Republican Governor Andrew Curtin, who guided the state through the conflict, remained a staunch supporter of President Lincoln, as well as an advocate of measures to assist the state's military veterans and their families. Beyond the large number of troops the state provided, Pennsylvania also represented an important part of the nation's war economy. Numerous arsenals and factories supplied arms and equipment, while Philadelphia banks provided vital capital and the state's coal mines helped fuel the Northern war effort.[4]

Blair County provided its share of Pennsylvania's volunteers and draftees. A number of militia companies had been in existence in the county during the period between the Mexican War and the outbreak of the Civil War. Several of these, including the Altoona Guards, the Hollidaysburg Fencibles, the Juniata Rifles, and the Logan Rifle Rangers, were mustered into service at the beginning of the conflict. During the course of the war, more than fifty volunteer companies that ultimately joined the Union army were organized primarily in Blair County, with an additional eighteen companies of militia also seeing service. Among the regiments with a heavy Blair County contingent were the Third and Fourteenth Pennsylvania Infantry of 1861, both enlisted for three months, and later the 105th, 110th, and 125th Pennsylvania Infantry and the Twelfth Pennsylvania Cavalry. A significant event that took place in the county during the war was the Loyal Governors' Conference, held September 24–25, 1862, in Altoona. The meeting brought together representatives from fifteen loyal states to discuss current military and political issues. After passing a number of resolutions, the governors then traveled to Washington, D.C., to meet with President Lincoln.[5]

John Black was one of the thousands of Pennsylvanians who rushed to defend the Union following the attack on Fort Sumter in April 1861. Although he never specifically stated his reasons for enlisting, it is evident from his correspondence that he felt a strong patriotism and devotion to the Union. A biographical sketch of Black contends that his early life "was but poor preparation for the hardships of a soldier's life, but it is doubtful if the young teacher ever thought of personal discomfort when his loyalty to the Union impelled him to enlist as a defender of the same."[6] In his letters he frequently made patriotic statements revealing his impassioned devotion to the cause. In June 1861, for example, he referred to a female acquaintance as a traitor because she would not display the U.S. flag. The following year he commented on his desire to return home "with the honor of having crushed one of the wildest rebellions that ever cursed a nation since the sun set forth its light upon the earth."[7] Black frequently expressed his disgust toward those who would not enlist, stating that "all true and loyal Americans" should answer their country's call.[8] He criticized a friend for failing to serve, stating, "So long as there is an enemy aiming at the destruction of Independence, so long should all loyal men continue to be soldiers."[9] A few days later he commented that death would be preferable to "have tyranny with its destroying hand . . . rule over such a heaven favored nation like this."[10] Later in the war, he expressed hope for a furlough, but Black stated that he, unlike others, would never leave the army without proper authority, pledging to "cast neither shame nor disgrace on you, myself or relatives."[11]

Though Black's letters are not replete with expressions of hatred toward his Confederate enemies, a few bitter comments do appear. In June 1862, for example, he expressed his desire to assist his country in "freeing her soil of [the] feinds [*sic*] of the South."[12] A few months later he referred to Confederates as "accursed rebels" whom he hoped would soon give up.[13] He saved his harshest words, however, for when he described the Confederate treatment of prisoners of war. "Who would have thought ere this cruel war," he wrote in December 1863, "that any American citizen could ever become so utterly lost and degraded as to allow their fellow beings to starve, while it lay in their power to render aid. God forbid that it should ever be my lot to again fall into the hands of those inhuman and degraded wretches. Wretches I call them. Nay! They are *worse* than wretches. Rather call them *fiends* & *devils* in the *shape* of men."[14]

Coinciding with his deep desire to fight was his growing camaraderie with his comrades of the Twelfth Pennsylvania, which is a prominent theme in his letters. Civil War regiments were in many ways extensions of a soldier's community, serving as a substitute family and home. Regiments were the nucleus of the army. They functioned as a cohesive military community that forged relationships between the members of the rank and file and became the foundation for larger military formations. Though the Twelfth Pennsylvania Cavalry had a somewhat checkered history, Black was consistently positive about the regiment's men and service. Like many soldiers writing home, he refrained from engaging in disparaging remarks about his comrades, many of whom were his friends. "Lucky for me," he recorded in 1862, "we have a noble hearted and true souled set of boys."[15] Even later in the war, when writing of his desire to be at home with his new wife, he added, "I cannot say anything against the service, for I glory in being a soldier."[16] In virtually every letter, Black mentions the activities of other members of the regiment, demonstrating a close friendship with a number of his comrades. Particularly poignant are comments concerning casualties and those suffering from illness. In late December 1864, after receiving news that a friend and fellow member of the regiment had died at a Confederate prisoner-of-war camp at Andersonville, Georgia, he wrote of the soldier: "I could not help shedding tears when I heard of it. He was a particular & warm friend of mine."[17]

Another major theme throughout his correspondence is Black's relationship with his sweetheart and future wife. During his military service, John wrote scores of letters to Miss Susan Jane Leighty, whom he called Jennie. Jennie Leighty was a native of Duncansville, Pennsylvania, where she was born on July 21, 1837, the daughter of George and Sophia Walters Leighty. From the tone of even the earliest surviving letters, it seems obvious that Jennie and John had enjoyed a close relationship for some time. Over the subsequent years of separation, their feelings intensified, and on April 3, 1864, while John was home on leave, they were married.[18] In an 1862 letter, Black addressed himself to Jennie as "Your true friend and lover."[19] The following year he wrote longingly of Sundays at home "when we sat alone in the little Parlor, not fearing any one, but having all of our pleasures to ourselves."[20] Later that year he thanked Jennie for having "proven [to be] so true to me, while many a poor soldier boy left his home & girl about the same time that I did and long ere this their girls have proven false to them."[21] By the end of that year, Black had pledged his "undivided love" to Jennie. He looked forward to the end of his enlistment and the chance to spend more time with her.

The emotional intensity of Black's correspondence shows him forging a strong and romantic relationship with Jennie. Despite their time away from each other, the distractions, and physical discomfort, this relationship developed affectionately through correspondence, led to an engagement, and then to marriage. In the midst of heated and chaotic military operations, Black makes Jennie a prominent character in his war and thereby illustrates through his letters the various ways the Civil War altered or nurtured romantic relationships. Jennie, in fact, becomes almost as prominent in his letters as the military events of the war, revealing the romantic intensity of their relationship. Indeed, despite John and Jennie's physical separation, the war's brutality, and even John's near-fatal wound in 1865, the romance between the two endured and became stronger. As such, Black's correspondence reveals the conscious decision to maintain a world inundated by love and affection—just as much as he was forced to live in a world filled with hardships and bloodshed. Throughout the war, Black found himself torn between devotion to his country and devotion to his wife. And while Civil War scholarship illuminates the many ways Northern women sacrificed their loved ones to the cause of preserving the Union, the correspondence between Jennie and John suggests that not all women willingly did so. In fact, this tension affected Black's camp life, as he felt tremendous guilt over leaving home, which he reveals to Jennie when he tells her of his dream about her in December 1864. The emotional tension he experienced provides a window for understanding the inevitable confrontation between civil life and military life. Black's remorse about accepting an officer's commission, thus sacrificing the initial months of his marriage to advance his military career, was representative of the emotional tension many soldiers experienced in the struggle to balance devotion to family with devotion to the Union cause.[22]

Black appeared torn between his devotion to the Union, and with it his desire to remain in service until the war's conclusion, and his love for Jennie and his desire to be at home with her. By January 1864, he had determined not to reenlist when his term of service ended later that year: "I will quit soldiering and not reenlist, but return to my native County and State, and let others reenlist who think proper."[23] In the end his sense of duty overcame his longing to return home. In a letter, Black reminded Jennie that he had asked her permission to remain in the service: "Had you not said yes . . . I never should have reenlisted."[24] Perhaps a promotion to lieutenant played a role in his decision to reenlist. He later commented that he accepted the promotion with the understanding that he could resign his commission within a year. By that time, however, officer resignations were limited to those with disabilities, so he would remain in the service. Throughout the remainder of 1864 and early 1865, Black appeared torn over his decision. He held out hope, however, that the war would soon close. Just one month after their marriage and upon his return to the regiment, John wrote to his new wife: "I have parted with you six times all together, but the last time was the hardest to bear. I thought it could hardly be that I was to leave you after being married, but you know duty called me away, and it had to be done."[25] In early 1865, John's letters were filed with comments about his hope for a furlough before the start of the spring campaign. Unfortunately, on March 6 he sadly informed his wife that he would not obtain leave. Just two weeks later he would receive a crippling wound that would change his and Jennie's lives forever.

A final theme of importance is the significance of the Twelfth Pennsylvania's contribution to the Union military effort in the lower Shenandoah Valley. During the final months of the war, the regiment operated in and around Harpers Ferry, guarding the Baltimore and Ohio Railroad and securing the mountain passes into Maryland. The regiment's operations were vital in protecting Unionists and tracking down and combating guerrillas, in particular, John Singleton Mosby and his partisan rangers. While scholars have exhausted the history of Mosby's exploits in the Shenandoah Valley, few have focused on the units that sought to defeat his rangers. Black's correspondence detailing the exploits of his unit in these operations helps fill this void in military literature. And although Black's unit had a reputation for being unruly and undisciplined, the appointment of Col. Marcus Reno in the winter of 1865 provided the Twelfth Pennsylvania with the leadership necessary to manage the unit's successful occupation of the lower valley, which ultimately forced Mosby's Rangers across the Potomac into Virginia.[26]

For John Black, patriotic ideology and love of country, coupled with a strong sense of duty and honor, as well as a sense of loyalty to his unit and his friends and family, appear to be the primary motivations for his Civil War service. Though a few years older and more educated than many of his comrades, Black was still representative of the hundreds of thousands of volunteers who flocked to defend the flag at the beginning of the war, determined to destroy secession and preserve the Union. While *Leather and Steel*, Larry Maier's fine work on the Twelfth Pennsylvania Cavalry, provides a detailed history of the regiment and the 2,236 officers and men who served in the unit, it is hoped that this book will help personalize the regiment's wartime experiences by focusing on one man who soldiered with it throughout the war.[27]

Acknowledgments

The editors wish to acknowledge the Jefferson County Historical Association for permission to reprint the letters of John H. Black of the Twelfth Pennsylvania Cavalry, which were published previously by that organization. We are especially appreciative to John E. Stealey III of Shepherd University for his willingness to initially publish a portion of these letters in article form. We also would like to thank those who made available a photograph of John H. Black. Thanks is also due to an unidentified reviewer of this manuscript for bringing to our attention a letter by John Black in the possession of the Virginia Tech Library. Tim Orr of Old Dominion University also carefully read the manuscript and made invaluable suggestions that significantly strengthened the book. We are grateful for his attention to detail as well as his insights, which enabled us to see in Black's letters a significance that lay beyond the battlefield. Janet Perkins of Richmond, Virginia, assisted greatly in providing genealogical information on a number of the individuals mentioned in the letters. John Jackson and Aaron Purcell of Special Collections, University Libraries, Virginia Polytechnic Institute and State University, assisted us in obtaining permission to use a John Black letter from their collection. Scot Danforth has been a great supporter of this work from its inception, and for many years waited patiently for its editors to finally bring closure to the manuscript.

Introduction

The American Civil War certainly does not lack for published source material. Before the conflict had even ended, thousands of memoirs, biographies, and regimental and campaign histories were printed. Despite this outpouring, scores of new books are published each year, indicative of the fascination many Americans still have for the most dramatic and crucial of our nation's conflicts.

In recent decades, the publication of the letters and diaries of private soldiers has become increasingly popular in Civil War literature. Each soldier had a distinct perception of the war, making his observations unique among the millions of participants. The editors of the following letters make no claim that it will change the way the war is viewed or reverse long-held opinions of particular generals or campaigns. It is hoped, rather, that the John H. Black letters will provide one more small piece of understanding to the puzzle of the Civil War. They provide new insights into the brutal, confused guerrilla fighting that occurred in northwestern Virginia and the role the Twelfth Pennsylvania Cavalry played in the war. For more than a century there was no published regimental history for the Twelfth Pennsylvania. This changed in 2001 with the publication of Larry B. Maier's *Leather and Steel: The 12th Pennsylvania Cavalry in the Civil War.* While this fine work helps rescue the regiment from historical oblivion, at this date there remains no published collection of letter or diaries from a unit member, except for those written by John H. Black.

The John H. Black Collection consists of approximately one hundred letters from the Civil War period. Written almost exclusively from Black to his fiancée and later wife, Jennie Leighty Black, the letters represent a fairly complete record of Black's service with the Twelfth Pennsylvania Cavalry from 1862 to 1865. In addition, one surviving letter was written in 1861 while Black served in the Fourteenth Pennsylvania Infantry, a three-month unit organized in April of that year.

Coeditor David J. Coles obtained the Black letters from a Civil War documents dealer in 1984. Until recently most were owned by a private collector living in Virginia, though they have since been sold. Individual letters are in the hands of other collectors and one is held in the library of Virginia Polytechnic Institute and State University. The provenance of the letters prior to the 1980s is unknown. Most likely, they were given away, sold, or lost by the Black family upon the death of the daughters of John H. Black. It is known that several letters were purchased individually by other collectors, but it is believed that the correspondence on the following pages is a nearly complete collection of John Black's Civil War writings.

Not all of the following letters are reprinted in their entirety. Black commented extensively on personal matters relating to his family and friends. The editors felt that this information would be of little interest to the general reader and have deleted some of this material. Deleted portions of the letters are marked with ellipses. Punctuation has been silently added to the letters to aid readability, and capitalization has been standardized. The editors also have added paragraph indentations to Black's letters at appropriate locations and spelled out some of his abbreviations.

In all but a few cases, Black's spelling was left in its original state. Most of the identifiable people and places mentioned by Black in the letters are covered in the footnotes. Brief editorial narratives have been included throughout the work in an effort to provide a broad historical background to the war.

Chapter 1

1861

John Black would spend most of the Civil War in the ranks of the Twelfth Pennsylvania Cavalry. He did, however, have an earlier taste of soldiering. In April 1861, Black enlisted in the Fourteenth Pennsylvania Infantry, a three-month regiment organized when Northerners still thought the war would be short and relatively bloodless. The unit was formed at Camp Curtin, Harrisburg, with Mexican War veteran John W. Johnston of Youngstown as its colonel. Recruits flocked to the regiment, and "the outpouring [of patriotism] everywhere was at the flood tide."[1] Black enrolled in Company H, a group of Blair County residents under the command of Thomas Holland. He held the rank of corporal in the company, which was known as the Scott Rifles.[2]

The Fourteenth was mustered into Federal service on April 30. After a period of training at Lancaster's Camp Johnston, on June 3, the regiment proceeded first to Chambersburg, Pennsylvania, and then on to Hagerstown, Maryland, and the vicinity of Sharpsburg. From this latter location Black wrote the only surviving letter concerning his service in the Fourteenth Pennsylvania.

On July 2 the regiment, along with other Union troops under the command of Gen. Robert Patterson, crossed the Potomac River into Virginia. For the remainder of its brief service, the Pennsylvanians patrolled the area of Martinsburg, Bunker Hill, Charles Town, and Harpers Ferry, failing to encounter any serious Confederate resistance. At Martinsburg a group of Unionist citizens presented the men with a handsome new battle flag.[3]

While the Fourteenth remained at Martinsburg, the remainder of Patterson's force marched up the Shenandoah Valley. The Federals' goal was to prevent Confederate troops under Joseph Johnston from reinforcing Gen. P. G. T. Beauregard at Manassas Junction. The aged Patterson failed in his effort, enabling Johnston to reach Beauregard with reinforcements. The result was Union defeat at the Battle of Manassas, or Bull Run, on July 21, 1861.

Later in July, following the Manassas debacle, the Fourteenth Pennsylvania returned to Carlisle, Pennsylvania. The unit remained there until August 7, when, upon the expiration the men's term of enlistment, the unit was disbanded and the men were mustered out of service. Many soldiers of the Fourteenth ultimately enlisted in other Pennsylvania units that were being organized for three years' service.[4]

* * *

June 28, 1861
Camp Newton
4 miles from Sharpsburg, Md.
Dear Jennie:

The fortune was mine to receive your very kind and delightful letter some 2 hours ago, and for me to answer. It is pretty hard work today and were it not to you I would not write for a few days yet. For the simple reason that while going through some extra movements with case knives along with one of my "buddies" through a mistake and accident together I received a slight wound on the 1st finger of my right hand, which after being dressed, swelled somewhat and makes it almost impossible for me to handle a pen, which you can easily tell by noticing my writing, but it will all be over in a few days and then I can write as before.

Since I last wrote you we had moved our camp from about 1 ½ miles further and are now encamped in a very beautiful grove and have shade plenty and enjoy the camp better than the one we just left, for shade is preferable to sunshine especially at present. We are encamped one mile from the Potomac river, and just two miles from the camp of the rebel troops, but we do not feel uneasy for they are too cowardly to cross the river and even when we go to the river, why they, poor cowards, run like everything for fear that we will shoot them, but they have to carry themselves very straight for we are expecting every day to march to the river and cross, and then call and see them, and I only hope that they won't run, for we do really feel as though we must have a fight before our time is up, but if we do not, why we will have the consolation of saying that we have kept the rebels from coming across the river and destroying the property of the many union men in Maryland, for you must understand that there are any amount of union people here, even the poor slaves cheer for the Union.

You say that Ellen Toole[5] is a traitor, nothing more than I expected, for I really think that she is one of that kind that are always opposed to what every body else is in favor of. If she don't hang out the American Flag, why I won't attend any more of her parties, and more [than] that I won't call to see her anymore. If she don't change her mind why she will never get a man, and that would grieve her very much. Any person in this part of the country, who speaks a word in favor of the rebels, is immediately arrested and brought up to camp and placed under guard and tried and kept under guard until further notice.

Three deserters were brought into camp yesterday evening and are now laying in the guardhouse hobbled and handcuffed, and will remain there until tried and all probability they will be shot, which they richly deserve. James[6] is well and getting along finely yet. As regards your hearing about our Company enlisting again there is no foundation to the report, for we have all come to the conclusion to return home when our time is up. Were it not on account of one, I would not go home until the war is over, and that one is yourself, Jennie, I am getting along exceeding well, have not been sick an hour since I left home and never had my health better since I am in service. Harvest is at hand and the farmers are busy cutting grain, and I asked for a pass this morning to go out and help a farmer a couple of hours for sport but the old Colonel refused and so I did not go. . . .[7]

I received a letter from Skyles this morning and he says he is going to Altoona on the 4th of July and he intends to take Louiza and you along, providing you will go and my advice and entreaty to you is to go and enjoy yourself, for I will be very glad to hear of you going, for we will be very apt to have quite a time on that day, and I want to hear of you enjoying yourself very much for it would be good news to me.[8]

I feel very sorry when I hear that you do not enjoy yourself very well. In about 4 weeks more we will be through and then we will return home to see our friends we have left behind. My love to your Mother[9] and Louiza and reserve a good portion for yourself, and believe me to be your true friend and ever will remain so, God permitting.

John H. Black
14th Regt. Comp. Pa. Vol.
Sharpsburg, Md.
In care of Capt. Holland[10]

Chapter 2

1862

On January 24, 1862, twenty-seven-year-old John Henry Black strode into a Philadelphia, Pennsylvania, recruiting station to enroll in the newly formed Twelfth Pennsylvania Cavalry. Black's enlistment papers show that he was five feet seven inches tall, with brown hair and beard, blue eyes, and a light complexion. The recruit listed his occupation as teacher and gave his residence as Eldorado, Blair County.[1]

The origins of the Twelfth Cavalry, organized initially as the 113th Infantry and also known as the Curtin Hussars after Governor Andrew G. Curtin of Pennsylvania, dated from November 5, 1861. On that day William Frishmuth, owner of the Frishmuth Foundry in Philadelphia, received authorization to raise a new regiment for three years' service. Throughout the winter of 1861–62, the unit was organized and trained at Camp McReynolds in Philadelphia. The enlisted men of the Twelfth came from a number of southern and eastern Pennsylvania counties, with more than four hundred hailing from Blair County. John Black was in Company G, composed primarily of men from Blair County. Adam Hartman served as Company G's initial commander. On February 18, Black was appointed orderly sergeant. He remained with the Twelfth at Camp McReynolds until late March or early April, when he visited home on a brief furlough.[2]

In late April 1862, the Twelfth broke camp for Washington, D.C. The regiment's commander at this time was Col. Lewis B. Pierce of Bradford County, Colonel Frishmuth having resigned his commission on April 20 after a number of controversies. The unit remained in Washington for about one month, providing guard duty for the city and continuing its training. While in Washington the unit finally received its weapons, although it still lacked horses.[3]

The regiment was sent next to Manassas, Virginia, scene of the Union defeat of the previous year. From late May through August, the men trained and guarded the Orange and Alexandria Railroad and the southern and western approaches to Washington. John Black and Company G were stationed primarily in the vicinity of Pope's Head Run, about eight miles from Manassas. Not until July did the cavalrymen obtain their mounts. The troopers were able to receive only rudimentary horsemanship training before they found themselves in combat. A historian of the Twelfth noted that "little progress . . . [was] made in training and discipline before active operations commenced."[4] The men would shortly have their baptism of fire.

* * *

Camp McReynolds,
April 9, 1862
Dear Jennie:

According to promise and in order to be punctual and have duty attended to, I this evening will write you a letter and give you a full history of my travels and arrival in camp. On Monday after bidding you adieu I went home, and at 11 in the forenoon I went to Altoona with Martin and Alex and saw them off. I then went home and called on Sam & lady. I spent several hours with them and then made my way home and went to bed and as you are well aware I naturally would take a sound sleep, for certain reasons.

Tuesday morning I rose early and took the 7 o'clock train and moved on towards Philadelphia. When I came within 8 miles of Harrisburg, I met Martin & Alex, and so I got off and went with them over the Susquehanna river to the town of Dauphin and took dinner, after which we paraded around through town and made quite a number of calls, among which we called at Mr. Winns' and got acquainted with his two beautiful daughters who entertained us very nicely for several hours. We then bade the folks good by and went to the station and by 5 o'clock we got aboard the train and away we went for Philadelphia. We arrived in the city by 11 o'clock and put up for the night.

This morning we came to camp and found all the boys in good spirits. Snow is as plenty here as at home. The boys were glad to see me [and] I in return to see them. This has been a very disagreeable day. Snowed and sleeted all day, and this evening it is stormy and sleeting at a great rate, but I hope that by morning the air will be calm and the day fair. So soon as I came to camp I was put to work, and had to make the payroll for the Company, still I took it all patiently and did as I was told and purpose [sic] doing so, so long as I remained in the Army.

I received your letter today but as you told me, I found nothing new, as you were kind enough to tell me all it contained before I left for camp. Evans[5] & Jacob Walters[6] send their respects to you. I gave the medallion to Barney[7] and told part of the old lady's story but could not remember it all. I feel very well today but not able to handle the saber. Still I think that in a few days I will be as stout as ever, and one of the busy bodies of the Camp for such I wish to be.

Well Jennie to tell the truth is my motto all the time and it is what is always requested. This is the third time that I bid you adieu within one year and the last time was the most sensibly felt, any how by me. It is hard to part with dear friends, but when duty calls I must obey, and hope for better times in a future day. Still Jennie be contented and be assured that I am among the living and well and feel perfectly at home.

Give my love to Lue and my best respects to your mother and Aunt and all the others you see. If any persons ask you what position James Irwin[8] holds, you can tell them that I saw him standing guard today as a private, and he is nothing else and more than that. He will not be any higher. . . . I will send the likeness as soon as I get to town to get it taken. So no more but take the high privilege of signing myself your most affectionate friend until death.

John H. Black
Ord. Sergeant Comp. G

Address the same as before and write soon.

Thursday morning April 10, 1862. Snow in camp this morning one foot deep, so we will have nothing to do today but shovel snow.

* * *

Camp McReynolds
April 14, 1862
Dear Jennie:

Here I am in Camp and have the good pleasure of acknowledging a very kind and lovely letter from you this forenoon. It gave me great satisfaction to hear that you are still among the list of healthy, But it makes me feel sorry to hear that you passed such a discontented week since I left, but still I feel glad that I have a friend at home that takes such great interest in my welfare, and for your sake I will take the best care imaginable of myself, and live in hopes that the day will ere long arrive that I will be permitted to see the rebellion ended and all of us soldiers return to our friends never to part while life remains. I have the privilege of telling you that I am again as healthy as ever and am attending to duty as before.

The snow has left and our Camp is very nice and dry. On Saturday last we went to the woods and got poles and spruce and made arches and wreaths for our Camp and everything has the appearance of home. We have been put down to duty in full. We have to drill some 6 hours each day, and have great difficulty in getting out of Camp. But still on tomorrow I am to have a pass to go to the City and then I will get my likeness taken and send it to you for your special benefit, with the firm belief that you will take the utmost care of it till I return to Blair County for good.

Yesterday being Sunday our Camp was full of citizens, and Oh! what a number of ladies were in to see us. We used them as well as we knew how, and invited them to call again, Alex is still with us and will not return home for two weeks. He is well pleased with Camp life and enjoys himself exceedingly well. Evans & Jacob Walters received your respects with pleasure, and join in sending their regards to you with the news that they are well. Barney is getting along well. You may tell Mrs. Engle so.

I am not surprised to hear that the people of Duncansville thought you and I were married and more than that I do not care what they think for my part. Indeed they must be very foolish to think that I could not stay over night with you, without being married. When any person asks you again about us getting married just tell them what you think proper and it will be all right with me. You will not do anything I know but what will please me, for it will be hard for you to displease me.

Give my best respects to Sue and tell her I am well and am busy all the time.[9] My best respects to your mother and tell her that I often think of her while I am in Camp. When you write again you need not use Col. Frishmuth's name for he is no longer a Colonel.[10] I will give you the address below, as it is changed. Take good care of yourself and trouble yourself as little as possible about me, for I am all right. My best love to you and I remain yours as ever with great respect.

John H. Black
Camp McReynolds
811 Noble Street, Phila
In Care of Captain A. Heartman
12th Cavalry Regiment

* * *

Headquarters 12 Regt. Cavalry
Camp McReynolds
Co. G
May 15, 1862
Dear Jennie,

Your letter reached me about a half hour ago and I was greatly pleased to hear that you are well and getting along finely, but I was very sadly surprized to hear that you did not get that picture. I had it taken put up in a gutta percha case and mailed to you with the letter and you say the letter reached you but the picture did not but hope that by the time this comes to hand that you will be the happy possessor of the picture. So I hope it may be.

We are still in Camp near the City of Washington and have orders to move to Virginia Saturday next, but such orders are all in my eye. My opinion is that we will lay here for a month or two yet. That is if we are not sent home before that. I am still well and enjoying myself exceedingly well. I can not say much about the regiment at this time for we have been laying idle for some days past, all on purpose to meet the paymaster with a hearty welcome. Jacob Walters is sick but says he is getting better, and before another week no doubt he will be ready for duty.

Jennie I am really sorry that your aunt got the varioloid but hope that she is by this time entirely rid of it. So our good friends are still afraid of you.[11] I find no person in camp afraid of me on the account of

9

the disease and further we have no Smallpox in our company or regiment so far, at least not so far as I know. Give my respects to all my friends about there and my love to Sue.

I was over the river a few days ago and took a look at the city of Alexandria and saw the house where Col. Ellsworth[12] was killed, and I had the pleasure of taking dinner with three of my [word illegible] friends in that City, James McIntosh, Uriah Benton and Henry Christy.[13] Evans sends his best respects to you. Barney is not very well but still not dangerous.

Well Jennie as the mail is about leaving I will close hoping that you are taking very good care of yourself and further that before two more months roll around I hope to be at home for good, for I think I am a good way for it. So with my best love I wish I will sign myself your ever true friend as before.

> John H. Black
> Address same as before

* * *

Pope's Head Run, May 31, 1862
Head Quarters of Company G, 12th Penna. Cav.
Virginia
[Dear Jennie:]

It is my great delight and high privilege of acknowledging a kind and interesting letter from you, on today; and in due reverence to yourself and your humble friend, I will immediately answer it, and send it by Monday's mail, which is the next that leaves our post office at Manassas. I am highly pleased to hear that you are right well again, and busy at your work; and I hope to hear such favorable reports from you during my stay in Uncle Sam's service. . . . It relieved me very much to hear that my likeness made the landing and also that it is highly prized by you. . . .

On Friday the 16th of May, the Paymaster came around and paid us off, and on Sunday following, we left Washington, got aboard a steamboat, and sailed down the river 6 miles, to the city of Alexandria, where we stayed all night. The next morning, we got aboard the Manassas Railroad cars and winded our way to Manassas, and after laying there about 24 hours, we went back on the railroad 8 miles and took charge of near about 4 miles, which we have to guard from the Secessionists, and we purpose [sic] taking good care of the road so that the bridges shall not be burned or the track torn up. Our post is not any ways dangerous at present, although it was a few weeks ago. But when we made our appearance the rebels left, with the exception of a few scudling [?] around through the wood, occasionally. Some of the boys of our regiment have captured some rabid secessionists, 12 in all, so near as I can hear. We have been fortunate enough to capture three horses, 2 foxes, 2 crows, 4 rabbits and 2 dogs, and intend to keep them as pets.

I have not seen Jacob Walters since I came to Camp the last time. He was put in [the] hospital at Washington and we left him there when we came to our present Camp, and I heard a few days ago that he has been discharged and sent home, and I hope it is so, for I think that after a person is compelled to go to the hospital he had better be discharged. I can stand soldiering with contentment for so long as health remains, but when it comes to going to the hospital I want to go home. But thank God I am as yet among the list of healthy and hope to serve my time out so. . . .

The war is moving slowly and we are not gaining much ground, but still we are gaining by degrees. It is not known how long we will be kept on this road, it may be for months, or till our time is up, and we may be called away before another week. The situation of troops is very uncertain. One day we may be here and the next away off at some other point. I am much obliged to those friends of mine who wish I never may return home, but I am under the impression that their hopes will be blasted. . . .

Our duty is not very hard. We have plenty to eat, although we have to break and eat hard crackers, as we had to do on last Summer. They take very well and I am fond of them. Our company is pretty healthy. We have only 6 sick, and two wounded by accidental firing of Lieut. Colonel Kohler of our regiment on Sunday a week ago. I will tell you more about the shooting when I see you, and give you the full particulars [of] how the two men happened to get shot. The fault lies in the hands of [the] Lieut. Colonel.[14]

Well Jennie I hope by the time this reaches you that the other letters will also be on hand. So Dear Jennie take good care of yourself, content yourself and pass the time as fast as possible and live in hopes that we will all be at home safe and sound. . . . Well Dear Jennie accept my best love, true regard and believe when I say that my mind often wanders to the dear little room where we spent many happy hours together and hope to spend many more. Your true friend and lover.

John H. Black

* * *

Wednesday June 4, 1862
Dear Jennie:

I wrote you a letter yesterday evening[15] and intended to mail it this morning but as it rained all forenoon I could not get it to the office. We have to carry our letters eight miles to the office and we send some one every day. I mostly go myself, But today no one would venture, and as I generally go on the cars, I could not go today on account of no trains running up. So I will drop you a few more lines and if you have to wait one day longer why you will surely receive a more extended letter which will suffice.

I am still the possessor of health. I am getting as fat as I used to be and am quite lively and joyful in the wild country and beautiful scenery of old Virginia. I am so taken with this place that I could content myself to live here all the days of my life. About the next thing you hear will be that I have bought a home and have retired to private life. That is no doubt you will hear it, but that is not say that it will be so. . . .

As it quit raining this afternoon I took a stroll over the hill (remember I had my carbine on my shoulder) and happened to find myself a beautiful meadow where I was lucky enough to find a host of the most delicious strawberries I ever set my eyes on. I was not long at gather[ing] a quart and making myself home to Camp to the Sugar box and there I had a mess, enough to make a Queen's mouth water. Oh! Jennie how would you have liked to be on hand at that time, to help devour the dear little berries, all buried in white sugar taken out of Uncle Sam's Sugar box.

Well Jennie as duty calls me two miles down the road to Sangster Station[16] I will have to close with my warmest regards and really true affection to a creature of my admiration and future happiness.

John H. Black
P.S. Tell Lue that I sent my best respects to her and her near friend

* * *

Pope's Head Run
Head Quarters of Company G
June 12, 1862
Dear Jennie:

. . . I am one of those of our gallant Company that can still rejoice in the fortunate possession of a due portion of good health. I am able for my rations, and trust that I may remain so. As each day rolls around I become more attached to our present scope of country and love to spend the days in roaming around and when occasion affords, I meditate upon the many happy hours I spent in Blair Co. Pa. until I become entirely absorbed in that topic and time. I then proceed upon my journey and throw away all thoughts of such topics for a few hours and become as jovial as before.

There are some few among us, who at times get to thinking about home and get in a very deep study and continue on at such vague studies until they become so overtaken with the study that it is beyond impossibility to drive it from their minds. And the result will follow in a few days that they are sick, and all brought on by too deep study about home. But if ever I should take sick while in the Army be assured that such is not the cause of my sickness, for I have so much control of myself that when I find I have studied enough upon a thing that I can for awhile drive it from my mind, and so should any sane person.

There is nothing that will bring a person to the grave so soon as homesickness, and how easy it is kept off if only time is taken by the forelock. The only cure for such disease is to form the unbroken resolution to take the world as it comes, and that too as cheerful as nature will allow one to do. Dear Jennie: You give me very unwelcome news about Skyles, nevertheless I believe every word of it, for it is nothing more than I often told you, and had good reasons to believe. I do pity him that he will not cast away that loathsome appetite for strong drink, when he really knows within his own heart that if he continues on, that it will bring him to utter ruin and also those with whom he may be connected to for life. Many a time have I shed tears, while alone, for our Dear friend Lue, for I well know that she is a true hearted Girl and one in whom any person who is acquainted with her and treats her with the treatment due a young lady, will find a never faltering friend. . . .

Oh! how I would love to occasionally have a pleasant chat with you both, But I must still obey my country and assist in freeing her soil of [the] feinds [sic] of the South, which I am confident we will have done in less than another year. So I consign myself to my duty and its cheerful as [a] morning bee. Tomorrow I purpose visiting Bull Run battle grounds[17] again and may give you some new and interesting sentences in my next letter. My best respects to your Mother and Aunt, and tell Lue to make a real good boy of Skyles, or I will have to tell them I cant be with them all the time. So with my Love to you, I sign myself, while I bid you good by, your true and ever affectionate friend until death.

> Sergt. John H. Black
> Company G
> Address as before

* * *

Pope's Head Run
Head Quarters of Company G, June 20, 1862
Dear Jennie:

As the evening is cool, leisure time is at my command and I having thoughts of home and of my home at different places, I will, by the light of my beautiful candle, make a feeble effort to pen you a few brief sentences. . . .

As my superior officers chose this day for themselves to visit Manassas, it fell my duty to stay in Camp, which had the tendency and effect of keeping me for one day from the beautiful cherry orchards, But lucky for me we have a noble hearted and true souled set of boys, who are always obliging. Some of them went on a cherry occasion today and on their return brought back with them a host of the delicious fruit, which they gave to me, at my disposal, and you may rest assured that I helped myself.

I am still enjoying excellent health and good spirits and am yet in love with this romantic country around us, And think that the love for the place will follow me whither so ever I go, for when duty calls me from here to others not so lovely I will no doubt be led to allow my mind to wander back to the pleasant and happy days spent in this Camp. Good news have I to write to you on this occasion. On yesterday afternoon Jacob Walters Came from the hospital and reported himself fit for duty. He looks very well and says he was very well treated while in the hospital. I was really rejoiced to see him once more, for I had entertained the idea that I would never more see him. He has not received any pay yet, but as payday will be around in about a day in about two weeks again, he will receive the full amount due him at one time. On tomorrow, if I be well, I will go to Manassas to see Capt. David Gardner, Lieutenant Henry Beamer,[18] and a few more of my acquaintances in that Company. They have been at Manassas for some two or three days, and no doubt I will have a gay time with them for a few hours at least. In my next I well give you an account of my visit to the gay boys.

Sam Evans sends his best respects to you and says he is well and in the height of enjoyment in Camp. The boys of our Company are all well but one, and he is fast recovering and will soon be on the duty list among his fellow comrades in Camp and speedily may it be. The 4th of July will soon make its appearance among us and we purpose giving him a hearty reception and do him reverence in a jovial manner. How do you intend to spend the day? Old Abe Lincoln passed here, on the cars, yesterday, on his way to Manassas, to pay General McDowell[19] a visit, and did not think worth his while to call on us. Never mind, we will serve the old chap the same sly trick when we pass through Washington once again. . . .

Well Jennie, night is fast passing away and the time to put out lights is being made known by the shrill tones of the Bugle, and so I must, with a few words more, close and bid you adieu again. . . .

So with my best and truest Love to you Dear Jennie, I sign myself your ever to be devoted admirer and truly affectionate friend while a spark of life remains.

John H. Black
Ord Sergt Comp G
12th Pa. Cavalry

Direct as before,
Excuse all you find amiss: Out goes the light for the night

* * *

Pope's Head Run 8 miles From Manassas
Head Quarters of Company G.
June 26, 1862
Dear Jennie:

On this beautiful and pleasant day, as the sun is throwing forth his refulgent rays, It is my privilege of acknowleding [sic] your welcome epistle of the 18th, and I will endeavor to answer it in the most appropriate style. . . .

I am in excellent health and am at all times ready for my rations and my duty. My duty at present is very light. It takes me but one half hour each day to perform it, and the remainder of the day is at my own disposal. I have told you frequently about our strawberries and cherries, and do not be taken on surprize when I tell you that the Mulberries are ripe, and that they are very plenty. It will not be very long any more until our large crop of peaches will be fit to gather and eat, and we are the boys for them. We have rain plenty with us. It rains about every other day. . . .

I hope that you . . . have a pleasant fourth of July, wherever you should happen to be on that day. As we are scattered along the railroad we do not intend to have any extra time on that day, and so will have to permit it to pass away almost unnoticed. Jacob Walters sends his best respects to you and says he is well. Likewise does Sam O. Evans. The boys of our Company are in excellent health with the exception of two who are unfit for duty, and they are not dangerous.

Our First Lieut. T. S. Shannon[20] has resigned and gone home to Philadelphia. No tears were shed when he left, except a few for joy. We have tired of him ever since the Regiment landed in Washington and we were not slow in telling him, so he thought he had better resign and leave us. Milton Funk[21] has been appointed to fill his place. He is the man that was to have it, when the Company was first organized, but through some sly trick of the captain he did not get it then, but now he is all right. . . .

Well Dear Jennie news is very scarce with me today and so you need not expect a lengthy letter. So with my best *Love* to you and advice to take care of yourself and not work too hard while I am away. I take the high liberty of signing myself your devoted, true and affectionate friend as ever, and ever will continue to be so.

John H. Black
Ord. Sergt. Company G
12th Pa. Cavalry.

Jennie: Hope, trust, be cheerful and contented as well as nature and circumstances will allow in time of Rebellion.

J. H. B.

* * *

Pope's Head Run, 8 Miles from Manassas
Head Quarters of Company G
July 1, 1862
Dear Jennie:

On yesterday evening I had the good favor of receiving answers from you to four letters and Oh! what an amount of news I then had and that welcomely received too, and so today I must get to work and answer all at one time. Glad tidings to me it is that you are still in good health, but some how or other you still say that you are discontented and down hearted, and think you will remain so, so long as I remain in the Army. Pity for you but it cannot be helped especially at the present. . . .

I am not surprised to hear of people thinking that we are married, if you keep yourself as close as you say, which no doubt you do, But just let them talk and think as they please and also do as they please. It requires time to disclose all things, and so what benefit can they gain by judging. I don't think that any of them would either gain or lose by it, if we were married or should even happen to be at some future day. Do you not think so? You may think I say a great deal upon that subject, but you must recollect I am prone to such errors, and if I should speak beyond bounds, why just you Dear Jennie excuse me for my folly and next time I will be better. . . .

My respects to your Mother & Aunt and all inquiring friends. Henry & Barney Engle are both well and doing fine. You have so often asked what was the matter with Jacob Walters. The Doctor says it was the Chronic Bronchitis, caused by practicing on the Bugle. He has quit playing the Bugle because he can not stand it. Well Dear Jennie as this is our mustering day and I am kept very busy on such days I will ask you to excuse this short and hasty letter. . . .

John

* * *

Pope's Head Run, 8 miles from Manassas
Head Quarters of Company G 12th Pa. Cav.
July 5, 1862
Dear Jennie:

 . . . The best news to you in regard to myself is that I am in the midst [of] the best health I ever enjoyed. I believe I never felt healthier than I am at present. The 4th is past and gone, making the second one that I spent in the service of Uncle Sam, and the Lord above only knows how many more I will be called on to spend ere this rebellion is crushed. I hope they will be few. I spent the day in Camp for the simple reason that the Captain and Lieutenant[22] went away in the morning and left me in charge of the Camp, and consequently I could not leave. Some of the "Upper ten"[23] of Washington and Alexandria went to Manassas in the cars and had a grand picnic and there is where the head officers of our Company we to be found. I understand they had quite a magnificent and pleasant time of it, while I was doomed to wile away the day in the lonely and almost desolated camp on that day, as most of the boys were gone.

Sunday morning July 6, 1862.
Dear Jennie,

I did not get my letter finished yesterday evening and so I well endeavor to complete it this morning. The sun in shining very hot upon us today. This is about the hottest day we have had since we were here, and I don't imagine how it could be any hotter if it would try. The only talk with us is how the great battle at Richmond will end, and which of the great Armies will come off as victorious.[24] I am still under the impression that McClellan will gain the day and by that the war will soon close, and all soldiers be permitted to return to their dear and beloved homes with the honor of having crushed one of the wildest rebellions that ever cursed a nation since the sun first sent forth its light upon the earth.

Your speaking of picnics and parties makes me wish I were there to attend them, for you are well aware that I am a lover of such things, But as I know I can't be there, I take the world as it comes and enjoy myself with it. Jacob Walters & Sam Evans send their best respects to you.

Give Lue my love and tell her to persevere and continue on persevering with Skyles, and she may eventually win him over to her kind graces and true affections. That is I say she may, not knowing whether she can or not. I think that all young men like Skyles that have or pretend to have the good of their beloved country at heart, as all true and loyal Americans should have, should at once answer the call of the Governor and the President for more troops, and show their loyalty by falling into ranks and enlist under the Stars and Stripes of their country. So long as there is an enemy aiming at the destruction of Independence, so long should all loyal men continue to be soldiers. For where is the true Unionist that would wish to live in this country when the Stars and Stripes should fail to wave over him.

Your devoted friend
John

* * *

Pope's Head Run,
Head Quarters of Company G
12th Pa. Cavalry,
July 10, 1862
Dear Jennie:

On this cloudy and rainy evening It was my good and delightful privilege of receiving another of your highly interesting, and at the same time truly welcome letters. . . .

So you spent the Fourth at home in quietude, and about the same way it was passed away by me as you will plainly see in the letter sent to you some four days ago, and I had a good reason for spending it in the way I did, for when a person is acting soldier, he does only as he can, and not all the time as he would desire. Still I was content, for I consider

I was fully as well off as they who went away early in the morning and did not return to Camp until three or four hours after the sun had gone down behind the western mountains.

We have been lying here in the present Camp so long already that we have almost come to the decided and fixed conclusion that we will stay for a considerable longer time, and in view of that belief, on yesterday, hot as the day was, we got to work and built a very nice oven and calculate to get a baker and then have fresh bread all the time we will be permitted to stay here, But I would not be a particle surprized, if by the time we have all things in good working order, that an order will reach us from the War Department to pull up stakes and forward march to some new destination, for a soldier knows not one day, where the next day will find him. One thing is certain we are all the time ready for any orders, that may and can be issued for us as soldiers, for we are here for duty and will obey at all hazards. . . .

And so in conclusion . . . I take the Liberty of signing myself with my best Love to you as your true and devoted friend as ever.

John H. Black

* * *

Pope's Head Run,
8 miles from Manassas,
Head Quarters of Company G
12th Penna Cavalry
July 20, 1862
Dear Jennie:

On yesterday evening shortly before nightfall, I had the pleasure of another very interesting letter from you, and I was pleased to hear that you still class yourself among the healthy, but I am the same time compelled to give you the sorrowful news that it is not my good fortune to be well, but am classed among the sick and unfit for duty, and have been so for three days past, but hope that it may not continue long in that way. My disease is not a very fatal one but it is real unhandy and troublesome. It is nothing short of the ear ache in its worse stage. It [is] so very painful that I can not sleep and have not slept a moment for the last two nights and as yet it is no better but I rather think the healing will break before night and then all will be right. My ear is swelled very much, but I am bound to bear it patiently a few days yet.

Our boys are kept very busy since we received the horses[25] and I am slightly inclined to believe that our easy times are about at an end and that we will have any amount of duty to perform, and further I think we will soon be called away from our present and delightful Camp and be sent to some post further South, for now we are well and fully equipped and nothing to hinder us from being called out immediately and placed in a more precarious position. . . .

The weather is very warm and the sweat rolls very freely down the cheeks of the soldiers, especially when called out on drill. . . .

Sunday evening. I am getting somewhat better this evening and hope that before this reaches you, that I will be able for duty. . . .

So I will close my letter by signing myself your ever true and affectionate friend

My best Love to you,

John

* * *

Pope's Head Run,
8 miles from Manassas
Head Quarters of Company G 12th
Pennsylvania Cavalry.
July 24, 1862
Dear Jennie:

As I wrote you a letter a few days ago telling you that I was not well, I must now give you the good news that the "ear ache" is now over and that I am once more classed among the healthy of Company G and trust that it may always be my good lot to give you such news. It is no very pleasant thing to be sick at home, but far more unpleasant to be sick and in Camp at the same time. I have no reason to complain of sickness for the Ruler of all earthly and heavenly things has dealt very lenient with me so far. Many others are afflicted for months after months while my term was of short duration here.

On yesterday afternoon the Captain and Lieutenant's wives arrived in Camp and proposed sojourning with us for two weeks. It had a tendency to make the two officers put on their Sunday faces and look quite pleasant, But poor fellows like myself who are in the single list, have no wives to call to see us, and so we are compelled to wile away our time in Camp without such joyous meetings on such occasions. But still we are content with the world and take things as they present themselves to the human eye, and at the same time cast our care in Providence and trust to the dark and hidden future, and time will reveal all things to us.

Since we have received our horses, we are kept very busy at drill. We have to rise in the morning at 4 o'clock and straight way repair to the stable and attend to our ponies, curry, feed, and water and then to drill, but we now have the consolation of drilling on horse back, [and] we will soon be prepared to move farther South and meet the rebels, with powder, lead and cold steel, and if we should be so very unfortunate as to have to retreat under such circumstances, we have the consolation of having horses that will carry us speedily to the desired point.

I suppose there is quite an excitement in little Blair County about these times in regard to enlisting, since the President has made the demand for four hundred thousand new troops, and I hope that if they do not get to work and enroll their names immediately and fall into ranks to assist in defending the beloved constitution of our County, that they may be drafted and be compelled to fall in as true loyal soldiers of the Stars & Stripes of their country.[26] There are any amount of young men in Blair Co. that I would love to hear of being made to go and handle the musket to quell the rebellion, for the more soldiers we have the sooner the war will be over, and if Skyles shrinks from the present call I will regard him as one who is not a true loyal citizen at heart, for I cannot see why under the Sun any young man can stay at home, when his country is all the time calling with might and main for his help. Shame! Shame!! Shame!!! on all young men who will stay at home and think that life is dearer than a land of Liberty. My motto is give me freedom though it costs many lives, and if I should not be spared to enjoy it after the war is over, I still have the blessed consolation of being one among the number who so nobly volunteered to gain it. To crush this rebellion it will yet cost the blood of many, and many too who will not be forgotten for many years after, But far better for those who are at home to lose friends and relatives in battling for freedom, than to have tyranny with its destroying hand to rule over such a heaven favored country like this. . . .

I take the favored liberty of signing myself your ever devoted and truly affectionate friend
and ever will remain so.

John

P.S. Dear Jennie: Suppose you get your likeness taken in a small case and send it to me by mail and you will confer an invaluable favor upon me, for I would very much like to have it

Your friend John

* * *

Pope's Head Run
Head Quarters of Company G. 12th Pa. Cav.
July 28, 1862
Dear Jennie:

This evening I had the pleasure of receiving your letter and it gave me any amount of very good news and now I will answer it, as my candle is burning and one of my comrades is doing his utmost to disturb me, for the simple reason that I disturbed him a few evenings ago, but he may do his best and he can not keep me from writing for such noise has no tendency to draw my mind from my duty. I am glad to hear that you are well and now I have the good news to send you that I am as well as ever and have at last gotten entirely rid of that troublesome ear ache. . . .

News is very scarce with us. We are put down to 6 hours hard drilling each day and have three months set as our time to prepare for active service at which time we will be very well prepared. Our horses do not mind firing much. It is an easy matter to go in full gallop and fire off a pistol or Carbine. Our boys are very apt riders, not one has been thrown off yet while on drill and the horses will soon understand the sound of the Bugle and commands as well as we do. I never thought that horses would learn so fast. I delight in drilling with horses and would not on any condition be in an Infantry regiment.

Our boys are all well and getting along swimmingly well, and are as jolly as so many bees. If any of the boys in the neighborhood with whom I am acquainted with should happen to enlist under the new call of soldiers, please let me know. You asked me about Henry and Barney Engle.[27] Barney is with us yet and is well, but Henry walked off without permission on the 15th of July and I received a letter from him since dated July 21st, at which time he was in Philadelphia, and said he would be at home in a day or two, and all I can tell him is that he had better soon return to this Company or he will be marked a deserter and sent after, which fact will teach him a lesson not to go away again without leave. Barney is very uneasy about him and knows not what to think of his father's proceedings. You may tell Mrs. Engle as much of this as you think proper, and all if you please. . . .

It is very warm with us, almost too warm to go out on drill, but still we must go when the Bugle sounds or we would not be considered true soldiers.

And now in conclusion with my best and truest Love to you. I will sign myself as heretofore my truest and most pious regards as your true and affectionate friend and will remain so.

John of Company "G"

* * *

Pope's Head Run
Head Quarters of Company G, 12th Pa. Cav.
Aug. 17, 1862
Dear Jennie:

. . . I still have my name enrolled among the large list of healthy soldiers, and I hope that it may continue [to be] my privilege to report so, for soldiering is not very hard when health is possessed, but hard, hard, indeed is it for the soldier when he becomes afflicted and has to be dragged from one hospital to another, and led to endure it all. The boys of our Company are in excellent health and in extraordinary good spirits, and at the same time eager to perform any duty or order imposed upon them. To be among such an obedient set of men gives a person great satisfaction. I must in duty to the boys say that they obey through respect and need not through fear.

Here we are at the same identical Camp yet, that we have spent the last three months in, and no orders yet to leave, But I rather think the day and hour is near at hand when an order will be issued for us to pack and onward march. It is my candid opinion that ere another Sunday morning's Sun sheds forth his refulgent rays, that we will be many miles from here and the Lord knows where. Remember this is only supposition on my part, and I pray that it may be so. We have been here so long that a change of place, in my estimation, would be for the better. And so if you should receive my next letter from a different office do not be the least alarmed on my part.

It gives me great pleasure to hear of so many of the boys coming out in the hour of our country's peril, and I ever shall hold them in remembrance for their patriotism, and my prayer is that they may shortly be permitted to return home with the great satisfaction of having it to say that they assisted in quelling the most outrageous rebellion that ever disgraced a nation.[28] What under the Sun can be the reason why Skyles does not take courage enough to come out a defender of the Union. I think I must stamp him with the infamous name of a coward and just what he deserves, if he still remains at home. Why cannot he come out nobly and say without a faltering voice, "I love my country better than my life," and if needs be to suffer death for the Flag to wave over our nation in peace and harmony.

Dear Jennie: You spoke again of that likeness, all I will say with due respect and Love to you, is for you to choose your own time and date for sending it. I have so much confidence in your word, and in you, that I know you will send it as soon as practicable, and when you do send it I rest assured it will be sent with a true feeling and the sincere emotions of a true heart, to one that highly esteems and will never fail to Love you as the nearest and dearest friend on earth, and with that assurance I will rest content, while I remain a soldier.

A train load of the new Soldiers passed through here this forenoon and more are expected to day. I understand that all the new troops will be immediately brought to Virginia to drill and relieve the guards along the railroad, so that we who have been in service for so long already will be moved farther on, to some more important posts.

Give Lue and Sue my Love and tell them that I am the same kind of a boy I always was, and just feel as though I would like to have a chat with you all, but such a thing will not take place I think until the war is closed and soldiers discharged. . . . Please let me know with what [regiment] Captain James [Hammer][29] and the rest of the boys went, as I am anxious to know. . . .

And now in conclusion I will send my best Love to you, while I sign myself as heretofore your unceasing and ever devoted friend as ever.

John

* * *

Pope's Head Run, Virginia
Head Quarters of Company G 12 Pa. Cav
August 20, 1862
Dear Jennie:

. . . Little did I think on last Sunday evening when I wrote you the last letter that I would this, a fair Wednesday evening, have the privilege of inditing [?] this from the above named Camp. On Monday morning last we received order[s] to pack up immediately and report on horseback at Manassas. We were not long in obeying the command, so that by 10 o'clock we reported ready for duty. We then got orders to march to Leesburg, 60 miles from Manassas, and by the time we were about starting on our long march, our orders were countermanded and we [were] ordered to wait an hour longer for further orders to come. We then impatiently waited for the hour to pass by in order to be apprized of the new order, when lo! and behold! the hour glided by and we received the unlooked for orders to march back to Camp and make preparations to be ready to march at an hour's warning and so we have been lying ever since awaiting orders, and as yet none have reached us. Nevertheless we have to stick close to Camp, and not go out of the sound of the shrill tones of the Bugle.

I have no idea in the least where we will be destined when we leave here, and know not when we will leave, may be not for weeks yet, and may be tomorrow noon. You can easily see by that, the uncertainty of the soldier's destination. But let the orders come, we are here ready and willing to obey, both through duty and respect, for it is our delight to be moving about from place to place, But Jennie I would say to you as a friend indeed, not to place any confidence in any vague report that may be passing around through the country and trust that from me you shall receive a true account of things as they really transpire and that too as often as anything new takes place in Camp, as any new move made.

I am still in very good health and am glad to hear that you are likewise. I rejoice in you getting to some frolicksomeness to drive away discontentedness, for that is the only way to be cheerful and in good spirits. Do not trouble yourself too much about me, but trust and hope for the better, and live with the belief that when this war is over that God will permit me to return safe home to you unharmed and with honor, never again to leave on such an errand again, for when this rebellion is over, war will be at an end for many years to come.

So that fellow of a Skyles has returned from Harrisburg and could not have heart enough to enlist and shoulder a musket in defense of a country that gave him liberty. Silent contempt is all I have on his case, and that I think is sufficient. . . .

Poor Mollie Slayman,[30] so she has no beau yet, only what will the poor creature do. If she only had one in the army, she could have some slight consolation, at least, but she is so unlucky as to have none nowhere.

Give my Love to Lue & Sue if you see them and tell them I am well. Remember me to your folks at home and any others that make inquiries. . . .

Love to you and ever shall continue so while life and sense remain with me.

Your ever to be, and now devoted friend.

John

* * *

The Twelfth's period of pleasant, light duty came to an abrupt end in August 1862 with the opening of Gen. Robert E. Lee's Second Manassas campaign. After pushing Maj. Gen. George B. McClellan's Army of the Potomac back from the gates of Richmond earlier that summer in the bloody Peninsula campaign, Lee moved his army northward to face another Union army under Maj. Gen. John Pope. On August 26 the Twelfth Cavalry was ordered to scout for the enemy in the vicinity of White Plains. Company G was left behind to guard Pope's Run, while part of another company and the Eleventh New York Artillery defended Manassas itself. With Colonel Pierce ill, Maj. Darius Titus commanded the regiment during the ensuing campaign.[31]

On the evening of the twenty-sixth, Confederates under A. P. Hill attacked Manassas and, after a "sharp encounter," dispersed the small force left to defend the town. The main body of the Twelfth found itself trapped between Bristoe and Manassas by Confederate troops under Thomas "Stonewall" Jackson. One source states that Titus "determined to cut his way through, or sell his command at a severe rebel cost," while another claimed that the major "cho[se] the alternative of a Charge" and attempted to escape. In either event, the regiment was decimated by the Rebels, losing 260 men killed, wounded, or captured.[32]

The remnants of the unit retired toward Alexandria, where Maj. James A. Congdon, who was temporarily in command because Major Titus was believed captured, reported the disaster to General McClellan. The next day the Twelfth was ordered to cross the Potomac River and patrol the north bank from Chain Bridge to Edwards Ferry. They continued this duty for the following month.[33]

John H. Black was among those captured during the confused fighting around Manassas, although it is unknown exactly when and where he fell into Confederate hands. He and a number of his comrades were apparently quickly paroled by the Rebels. This practice was common during the early years of the war. Prisoners received paroles from their captors under oath that they would not fight again until properly exchanged for a prisoner captured by the opposing side. Black and his fellow parolees then traveled to Camp Parole, Maryland, a facility established to house paroled prisoners awaiting exchange. He would stay there until December 1862, when he was formally exchanged.[34]

* * *

Camp Parole
Annapolis Md.
Sept. 17, 1862
Dear Jennie:

Once more a highly welcome letter from you to me has made its appearance on my rough board table for since I am here I have made a table such a one as it is too. I was better pleased today in receiving a letter from you than I have ever been, on account of being so long without any news from you, and so now for an answer, such as it will be.

Jennie: it is highly delightful and cheering news to me to hear that our folks from home called on you and paid you a visit, and further that you say you are going out to see them. Just such news as that, is what I glory in hearing and my advice is continue on at the same thing and you will please me very much, I am in good health yet and rejoiced to hear that you are well.

It was nothing more than I expected to hear that news would go home that I was killed, but I was more fortunate than that although I was among the very unfortunate. It is not any ways lonesome here, for there are any amount of Paroled Prisoners here. The full amount in Camp so near as I can ascertain is about 8,000 altogether may be more and I am sure not less. We have no sign of being exchanged yet and fears are ascertained that we will have to stay here until the war is over. Oh! What a pity I say.

In the letter I wrote you a few days ago I said that there was some probability of me getting a furlough, but I cannot succeed and so I have given up, and will have to content myself with staying here until further orders, and that may not be until the close of the war. One thing I can say that we live well here and have gay times doing nothing and expect to being at that for some time. Give my Love to Lue & Sue and remember me to your mother and tell them I am well and getting along very well for a prisoner.

Nothing more as I have no more news. So Good by for this time with my best love to you as my truly dearest friend I possess upon earth.

Your friend indeed as truly as ever.

John H. Black
Direct as before

* * *

Camp Sangster, or rather "Camp Parole"
Annapolis, Md.
Sept. 21, 1862
Dearest Friend Jennie:

. . . I will give you the news that I am still enjoying very excellent health and so long as health remains I can make out to content myself in all other adversities as well as any other soldier, either active or paroled. Since I last wrote to you, about 11,000 more paroled men made their appearance in Camp, and so you may imagine that we have quite a gang of useless boys here, For we are all well aware that a paroled prisoner is of no use to the government except to draw wages & rations and at that we are all well at, But I would far rather be in my Company earning my wages and rations in doing service for my country. But so it is and cant be better.

I have not received a letter from the company since I have been captured and therefore I cant tell where they are and who is living and well. Rumors are afloat in Camp every day about the company but I credit none of the reports until I get the official news. In regards to Sam O. Evans getting wounded, I would not be the least surprized, but I never heard anything about it until you wrote to me about it. About William Gwin,[35] I cannot say whether he is killed or not. But one thing I have been informed of by a number of men who I can rely on confidentially, that one of our men was found dead two days after the battle. He was found about two miles from Manassas, and said to have the letter G on his cap. But as to whom it was I am not able to say.

I have [written] the Company several times for my Descriptive List and some articles I have with the Company but so far I have received no answer. Whether the Captain has received my letters or whether I am forgotten by them is hard for me to tell. I would very much like to hear from them for I am over anxious to know how they have been getting along since I was unfortunate enough to leave them.

So Skyles has taken that to himself that I wrote to Reeves,[36] and sure enough I intended it on him, and many more things I will have to tell him, if ever God permits me to return home. Tell Lue [Sue?] as she is somewhat taken with George Vaughn, that when Georgy returns at the end of 9 month's service, to please for the sake of her friend John, put off the wedding until the war is over so that I can be present at the grand festival, and then I will tell her the story of a Jackson Prisoner captured on the 26th of August at midnight and on the morning of the 29th of August at 10 o'clock was paroled and is now encamped at Annapolis, Md. subject to the orders of the government. So tell her that when I last saw her she was single, and that I want to have the privilege of greeting her as a single lady still and that I anticipate have some sport at her wedding. . . .

In order that you may know exactly whom of us are here of our Company I will give the names. William K. Hollis,[37] Richard Yost,[38] Patrick Burns,[39] Matthew Akin,[40] James Funk,[41] Barney Engle & John H. Black, 7 in number, and no more. We are all here and not a wound on either one, we are all healthy. . . .

So in conclusion, with my best and sincerest wishes for you, that your days in this world may be happy ones, and that if I never meet you on earth that we may meet in heaven where parting will not be known.

So good by for this time while I subscribe myself yours for life

John
Address as before.

* * *

Camp Parole,
Annapolis, Md.
Sept. 27, 1862
Dear Jennie:

. . . [I am] in very excellent health and in high spirits on account of the glorious victories achieved on the battlefield by our untiring troops under the gallant and excellent General McClellan. Would he have been in command of the last Battle of Bull Run our Army would have come off victorious, but as it was it did not, for General Pope has not had military experience enough to carry on a battle like that to victory, and I think it was high time that our government had the goodness to let McClellan direct the battles as he saw most appropriate,[42] And now with McClellan at the head of our great Army once more, I expect to hear of victory after victory until the accursed rebels are driven so far South they will not have any more foothold and will be led to exclaim that it is useless to combat any longer against the north, but submissively lay down their arms and offer themselves up to the north as a conquered rebel crew and be willing to live under the Stars & Stripes again.

I don't want you to trouble yourself so much about us Paroled Prisoners being formed into Companies and transported or rather transferred to the West to fight against a lawless set of savage Indians.[43] I am not, in the least, surprized that that report reached your ear, for it has been rumored here to some extent, and has also caused quite an amount of dissatisfaction among the soldiers in Camp. But at that point it stops, for it is and was only a rumor gotten up by some persons on purpose to raise an excitement.

Here we are as Paroled Prisoners, And ere we were Paroled we had to give our word and honor and many had even to take the oath that we would never take up arms [to] aid or abet the United States, against the Southern Confederacy until we are regularly exchanged, and any one can plainly see that if Paroled Prisoners (unexchanged) go out west and take up arms against Indians, that they will be aiding our government against the South. For if we should go out there, why those soldiers, who are now there would be relieved and taken down South and thereby strengthen our army against the South, to the amount of Paroled Prisoners sent west. And you can plainly see that such actions on our part would be conflicting with our word, honor and oath, and you well know that such a government as we have would never exact any such of a thing of us. Far be it from it, And so Dear Jennie as you place so much confidence in whatever I say, Take my word for it that so far there are no fears of us ever taking up arms again until we are regularly exchanged, and when that exchange takes place, why you may rest assured that instead of us going West, we will be sent to our Company and Regiment and then wherever the regiment moves why there we will be, But I, to express myself candidly I must say, that I fear that there will be no exchange made while the war lasts, And Oh! must I then lay in Camp doing nothing all the time, without having another opportunity of being a member in full of old Company G. No doubt you will laugh and say so much the better of you and me, but I can't say so, But surely let that all be as it will, and no doubt it will all be for the better. But one thing, don't you trouble yourself about me going West, for it is so far as I can ascertain nothing but a perfect hoax. So let content be yours, and rest easy and do not place any confidence in any more such reports.

We are getting along finally in this Camp, and if I am to stay in any Camp during the coming winter, I hope and trust that it will be this one, for here I can content myself as well as in any other Camp, under present circumstances. Here we get our rations as regular as clockwork. We get soft bread every day in the week except on Saturday, and for that day we have to take crackers. But the bread we get for the six days, lasts us for the week, so the crackers are an overplus [?]. Every other day we get fresh beef, and plenty of everything else all the time. I would not wish to live better than we live here, for we have every convenience for cooking and it is a poor cook that cant make good meals out of the allowance we get. The only thing we have any reason to complain of is that they are very slow in issuing clothing to us, but by having patience for a few days yet, we will be clothed as well as we were before we lost our extra clothing on the battlefield.

Give my Love to Lue and Sue and tell them that I am in good health and getting along swimmingly well, and have a gay time in Camp. Many scenes that have taken place in Camp here, I will leave untold untill I get to see you again.

> Yours forever and ever
> John
> Direct as before and it will
> reach me.

* * *

Camp Parole
Annapolis, Md.
Oct. 30, 1862
Dear Friend Jennie:

This is a very pleasant and delightful morning, and it is my good pleasure to have a letter from you, with the glad tidings that you are well, and to you I return the same important and good news of myself. So you are still discontented at times, nothing more than I can expect of you, but don't think I blame you for it. No dear, not at all for it is natural for a person to be so who has any feelings for a friend away from home under such circumstances. I believe you truly when you say you would like to see me, and so would I like to see you, but at present I can't afford you that great pleasure.

Along with your letter came another from a friend , giving me most painful news, but such is the fate of this horrid war. Sergt. McCaulley,[44] Sergt. Lehr,[45] and Brannan[46] of my company were killed in the last engagement the Regt. had. Poor fellows, so they have been ushered into eternity a sacrifice for their country. I did consider it a great misfortune when I was taken prisoner, but my fate was better than theirs, so I will cease to complain anymore, but let well enough alone.

We have had a hard time of it the last week in my little mess of 14 men, one of the boys of the mess, a member of Company E, is very ill, and is not expected to live. We have to be up with him night and day, he is entirely deranged. His wife is here with him, she came the day he took so bad. Poor fellow I wish he was at home, where he could be better attended to. Still we are doing our best for him, and better cannot be expected.[47] I do feel for a poor soldier sick in Camp, for the attendance is never half so as it would be at home. Good health is a soldiers choice fortune, and I thank the most high God that I possess such good health, for I have seen a number of sick since I have been in the army. The hospitals here are full all the time, but we can't expect anything else among so many men as we have here. The boys of my Company are all well. . . .

I am glad to hear that Gwin is at home, and if you get to speak to him, give him my best respects and tell him I am well and in Camp Parole. After court is over, give me all the particulars about Ellen Toole and her friends "over the left."[48] Times are good in Camp yet and sport as plenty as ever. We have a fiddle, fife, mouth organ and Jewsharp in our mess and when they all are in tune, we have a variety of music.

Nothing more but my best to you while I affix my name as your sincere friend until death parts us.

John H. Black

* * *

Camp Parole
Annapolis, Md.
Nov. 3, 1862
Dear Friend Jennie:

. . . It is always good news to me to hear of your good health and it is gratifying to me too that you are at times in pretty cheerful spirits. You appear to be very well pleased that an exchange of Prisoners is "Played out" and it does not surprise me in the least, for I know you that well to judge that you are honest in it too, and I do not blame you at all. Still I would far rather go back to the regiment than stay here, But since I know it can't be did, why I am content, for I always feel contented, and hope I always may. I am in good health and prospering as finely as any use in, in a Camp of Paroled Prisoners.

As winter is about setting in, we have made preparations for it. We have fixed our quarters as comfortable as possible. We bought a cook stove a few days ago and put in our well arranged kitchen and now we are getting up our meal according to the taste of all the squad. We live well these days. We have milk in our coffee every meal, we get it at the "*trifling*" price of 10 cents per quart. We draw molasses from the government and when we take a notion to have a little butter, we go up to the Sutlers and buy it at the "*moderate*" price of 30 cents per pound. . . . [49]

> Yours always
> and for ever
> John H. Black

* * *

Camp Parole
Annapolis, Md.
Dec. 1, 1862
Dear Jennie:

We have packed up all our affairs and will leave here in about an hour from this [place]. The Capt. is here already for us and says he will take us to the regiment. I am in good health and in great spirits, and you need not answer this until you hear from me again, which I hope will be in a few days, and that too from the Company.

My respects to all and my love to you.

> Yours forever and ever.
> J. H. Black

* * *

Soldiers's Retreat[50]
Washington, D.C.
Dec. 3, 1862
Dear Jennie:

About 15 minutes after I wrote that letter to you telling you we would soon leave, we left the old Camp and marched to the station. There we put up in tents until yesterday morning at 5 o'clock, when we got aboard the train and by nine we were safely landed in the City of Washington. We were then marched into the large eating room where we partook plentifully of Bread, Cold Ham and hot coffee. After that was over we marched to the barracks and are now in a large and comfortable room, with a huge stove in it.

How long we will remain here is hard to tell. It is here we must be full clothed and equipped for the battle field. I have an idea that we will leave within 10 days at least and the sooner the better, for my aim and desire is to be with the boys in the company at the earliest period possible. I am still in excellent health and am pretty busy too, as it requires some writing and running around to get along as ordered. The Captain is with us and as clever as a basket of chips. He treats me like a brother, and is in a hurry to get us back again. . . . [51]

I sign myself with pleasure yours forever and ever until death.

1st Sergt John H. Black
Co. G 12. Pa Cav
Soldier's Retreat
Washington, D.C.

* * *

Soldiers's Retreat
Washington, D.C.
Dec. 12, 1862
Dear Jennie:

On yesterday evening it was my good fortune to receive from you one more of your interesting letters. Did I say one? I should have said more, for I received three at the same time, and as they came together, I will answer them all in this one, which I hope will suffice for the present, with the promise that I will write again as soon as convenience will allow, which will be after my arrival at the regiment. We are still putting up in this abominable city, and I am in good hopes that we will soon leave. The order just came in that we are to start on our line of march on Sunday morning next. We will then have 156 miles to ride until we arrive to the town of Bath, Morgan Co, Virginia, where the regiment is now encamped and doing duty, and it is the general belief that we will stay there during the winter, and if so we well no doubt become somewhat acquainted before we leave. In this City I would not like to spend my days, for I have a mighty poor opinion of the place. Few harder places are to be found anywhere in the United States.

Barney is still with us and is in good health and so is your humble friend in good health, that is myself and also in good spirits and in expectation of soon having a happy meeting with the boys of my company, And God only knows when I will be permitted to have a happy meeting with you. Still I trust that the time speedily passing by and soon the last battles will be over and the soldiers be winding their ways to their homes which are dear to them, and to their friends that are ever dear to them.

So long as God permits me to enjoy good health, I can get along very well in the Army, but if affliction should be my lot, why then there may be different feeling come across my mind. . . .

So with my undivided and ever constant Love to you I close.

> Yours forever & ever
> will remain
> John H. Black
> Co. G 12 Pennsylvania Cavalry
> Hancock, Md.

Chapter 3

1863

When John Black returned to the Twelfth Pennsylvania Cavalry in December 1862, he found the regiment encamped at Kearneysville, Virginia, guarding the Baltimore and Ohio Railroad. For most of the remainder of the war, the regiment served in the lower Shenandoah Valley. The fighting there was very different from that in the major theaters of the war. Although the valley witnessed extensive combat and several large campaigns, much of the fighting was on a smaller scale, with scouting, patrol, and guard missions the most common type of activity.

The year 1862 had been active and not terribly successful for John Black and the Twelfth Pennsylvania Cavalry. Little military activity involving the regiment took place during the winter of 1862–63. Until April the unit remained encamped at Kearneysville and then near Winchester.[1]

* * *

Karneysville, Va[2]
On the Baltimore & Ohio R. Road
Camp Owl's Misery
January 8, 1863
Dear Jennie:

Snow has been flowing pretty freely all day and the weather is pretty cold for once, and has a tendency to make soldiers sit pretty close to the tent stoves. Our quarters are pretty comfortable. . . .

So our friend Sue is married at last, and no doubt is well pleased with her choice, and all the harm I wish her, is that she may live a happy life and never have a word out of the way in the Union, and that health and prosperity may be theirs both here and hereafter. Give my best wishes to them if you see them, and my Love to Lue and tell her to take good care of Skyles, and stick close to him, but tell her not to marry until I get home, for I want to see the knot tied.

No news of any importance with us, for we hear of no rebels being about our outposts, But there is no telling how soon they may show their grey clothes on our path. If they do we will fall in line and meet them as best we can. . . .

So Good by while I sign myself yours alway[s] to be and forever shall be.

John H. Black
Co. G 12. Pa. Cav.
Martinsburg, Virginia

Address at present

* * *

Karneysville, Va.
Camp Owl's Misery
January 16/63
Dear Jennie:

. . . By the heading of the letter you will learn that I am still at the same old place. My health and so forth, same as usual. Mud and rain is abundant and our Camp is in a miserable plight. Mud is deep and plenty to spare. Still we soldiers take it all as cool as a "cucumber" in harvest time. On last evening we received marching orders, to leave this morning at 6 o'clock, but ere the time arrived the orders were countermanded and so we are still here yet. Our duty is not getting any lighter yet, but we are the boys to stand it. I am pleased to hear that Bartley[3] has such a good opinion of his wife, and who wouldn't so soon after marriage. Let one year pass away and the second year passes and then we will hear the news of them and if the same Love exists there can be some confidence be placed in the reality of it. No doubt he will always think as much of her as he now does, and if so she has made a happy choice indeed. The next two years will tell many tales, to some they will be favorable and to others unfavorable with a reality. To you and myself I trust it will prove favorable.

The signs and times so far do not have a tendency to close this horrible war, and God only knows when it will end. The sooner the better for everybody I would say. . . . You speak of people sleighing. We have no snow, and if we had we could not sleigh for the reasons that we have no sleigh and could not get permission either. If you get any opportunity of taking a sleigh ride be sure and take advantage of it, and enjoy yourself, and I will find no fault in the least, For with you I never have found fault and hope I never may. Do not stay at home for fear of insulting me. But improve every opportunity to enjoy yourself and to it I will say all right, for I am not easily insulted, particularly by a girl whom I recognize as a true hearted, sensible, and loving young lady.

So with my best regards to your mother aunt & uncle dave[4] and my undivided Love to you I sign myself ever yours

John H. Black
Co G 12. Pa. Cav
Martinsburg, Va

* * *

Karneysville, Va.
Feb. 18/63
My Dear Friend Jennie:
About ten minutes ago, the mail carrier came into my tent and found me all alone, and said to me "John, I have a letter for you and it is from your Duck too" and on receiving it I found his saying to be about as near the truth as he generally tells. . . .

About you often getting almost out of heart on account of the continuance of this war, I am not a particle surprized at you, for there are many that feel likewise, but for myself I am getting in good hopes that this war will not last so very long any more, not over a year at the farthest if that long. In one year from now I expect to see the close of the war and myself at home with you, with the solemn vow that never shall be broken by me or you, "God's will be done" and not ours, Jennie. And so we will let the worse go with the better and take everything cool and with a resigning will and conscience. . . .

Everything is moving along quite smoothly with us, and we are passing the time swiftly. Our wounded man is recovering rapidly. He was in camp on yesterday to see us and thinks that he will soon be well again and fit for duty. The bullet came closer to him than I want one to me.

So George Slayman[5] has come down to hard crackers. We have the advantage of him in that so far, we have fresh meat, fresh bread, onions & potatoes along with our coffee and that plenty too. It is here that we live well, but how long it will last I cannot tell. We have had to eat cracker but one week since I returned to the regiment and well we deserve all those things, for we have three times as much duty to do as we ought to do, but we do it cheerfully and never complain particularly while we live so well. Good living is the half of what a soldier stands in need of, and then he can get along, it matters not what duty is imposed upon him. Did I tell you we were paid on the 12th of this month. It will be nothing wrong if I tell you this second time.

My love to you, my respects to all your folks at home. I will sign as before, yours forever and will be true.

> Yours forever
> and ever will be true.
> John H. Black
> Co. G 12 Pa. Cav
> Martinsburg, Va.

* * *

Camp near Winchester, Va.
March 22, 1863
[Dear Jennie:]
    . . . You complain about the Sundays and Sunday evenings being such lonesome times to you. Dear Jennie, I pity you very much on that account for I well know that you enjoy yourself very well many a Sunday & Sunday evening that has past and gone, when we sat alone in the little Parlor, not fearing any one, but having all our pleasures to ourselves. Alas! Dear Jennie, those days are past but I hope not forever. . . .

On yesterday two of our boys were brought back to Camp. They left us in January last on leave of their own and happen to be picked up by the authorities and were placed under Guard and then forwarded to the company. They are now in the Guard tent and who knows when they will be out. So much for going home without leave. . . .

> I remain yours forever true
> John H. Black, Co G 12 Pa. Cav.
> Winchester, Virginia

* * *

In early April 1863, Robert E. Lee authorized Brig. Gen. John D. Imboden to advance his Northwestern Virginia Brigade into Union-occupied West Virginia. Imboden's brigade, along with a separate force under Gen. William E. Jones, was to tear up the Baltimore and Ohio Railroad from Grafton eastward and to gather as many prospective recruits, provisions, horses, and cattle as possible. From Staunton, Virginia, Imboden moved westward to Beverly and Buckhannon. He threatened both Grafton and Clarksburg but found them too heavily defended. During late April and early May, a series of skirmishes erupted between the raiders and Union troops guarding the region. The Federal command called for reinforcements to drive out the raiders.[6]

Among the units dispatched to the area were elements of the Twelfth Pennsylvania Cavalry. Before leaving for western Virginia, the Twelfth was involved in a disastrous affair at Fisher's Hill. Along with a portion of the Thirteenth Pennsylvania Cavalry, the unit fell victim to a Confederate ambush, suffering heavy casualties. With the memory of this unfortunate affair still fresh in their minds, the troopers of the Twelfth were transported westward to a new theater of the war.

On May 5 the regiment participated in an expedition to Jane Lew, a small hamlet between Clarksburg and Weston. The Pennsylvanians, bolstered by portions of the First and Third West Virginia Cavalry, and the Twenty-eighth Ohio Infantry, skirmished inconclusively with Imboden's men. Several Rebels were captured, as well as a small cache of supplies. John Black would leave a detailed account of his affair in his letter of May 9. After the repulse of Imboden's raid, the Twelfth was sent to join the garrison at Winchester, Virginia. Within a short time, the regiment would again be in contact with the enemy.[7]

* * *

Bridgeport, Virginia
May 9, 1863
Dear Jennie:

The last letter I wrote you was dated April 30 [not in this volume] and no doubt you have been in a query why I have not written since. First I will tell you that I had not time and Second, if I would have written I could not have sent it ere today.

On the first day of May we ordered to proceed to Martinsburg, Va. and the next morning we and our horses were put aboard the railroad cars, and moved on speedily about 200 miles until we arrived in the western part of Virginia. We landed about 30 hours after we took the cars, [and] marched to this place. From here we went on to a town by the name of Clarksburg. Six companies of our regiment went some 12 miles farther over an awful muddy road, into hollows and over hills and mountains.

We stayed there three days and nights. We did some scouting while we were there. On one of our scouts we encountered 48 rebel cavalrymen, routed them entirely, killed 4, captured 5, wounded several and drove the remainder pell mell to the mountains. You should have seen them run and dodge the bullets. I never saw such a set of scared chaps as they were. They were so suddenly taken on surprize that they fired but few shots at us, and what they did fire, were only at random. We captured a number of their horses and arms. We returned to camp without the loss of a man or even wounded. I like this part of Virginia far better than at Winchester, and I hope we may spend the summer here, providing we have to remain in the army.

When we charged on the "rebels" in that little town of "Jane Leugh" the Union ladies were out in front of the houses waving their white handkerchiefs and cheering us. It made us feel really patriotic. The majority of the people about here are loyal, and truly loyal too, for they have armed themselves with muskets, shotguns, and all kinds of arms they could get hold of, and have gone into a regular "bushwhacking" game.

I am getting along fine and in good health and hope that this may ease your mind somewhat. I will write in a few days again, if we do not get on another such long march. How soon we will get in another skirmish I can't tell. We keep prepared all the time for the worst. My Love to Lue, and my best respects to your mother and aunt. And lastly but not least my Love to you while I sign myself yours

forever true
will be.
John H. Black
Company G 12. Pa Cav
Bridgeport, Va.
You need not answer until I write again.

* * *

Winchester, Virginia, was one of many Southern towns destined to be occupied by both sides during the course of the war. As key to the Shenandoah Valley, three major battles took place n the vicinity of the town. Throughout the first half of 1863, troops from the Union army's Middle Department defended the town. Maj. Gen. Robert H. Milroy commanded the nine-thousand-man force, which he felt was essential to guard the approaches to Harpers Ferry and to solidify control over the lower Shenandoah.

The Union high command, and particularly Maj. Gen. Henry Halleck, was concerned about leaving such a large force in a relatively isolated location. Halleck argued that Winchester was indefensible and should be maintained only as an "outpost" for the defense of Harpers Ferry. Several times he suggested to Maj. Gen. Robert C. Schenck, commander of the Middle Department, that the town be abandoned. Schenck unfortunately disregarded Halleck's suggestion.

In early June 1863, Robert E. Lee began moving his Army of Northern Virginia north from its camps south of the Rappahannock River, beginning his great invasion of the north. Led by Richard Ewell's Second Corps, Lee's army moved quickly around the Federal right flank into Shenandoah Valley. By June 12, Confederates had approached to within striking distance of the unsuspecting Federals at Winchester. A prominent historian of the Gettysburg campaign has written that the Union garrison "made a tempting prize for Lee, and it was only a matter of time before he would try to claim it."[8]

John Black and the Twelfth Pennsylvania Cavalry were among the ill-fated defenders of Winchester. On June 12, the regiment was sent out along the Front Royal Road to ascertain the enemy's strength. At this time General Milroy felt that only a small force of Rebel cavalry was to his front. At Cedarville, twelve miles from Winchester, the Federals ran into a large Confederate force. Lt. Col. Joseph Moss, temporarily in command of the Twelfth Cavalry, reported the contact to Milroy, who discounted the information. He still refused to believe that the main body of Lee's army had moved so far northward.[9]

Throughout June 12 and 13, desultory skirmishing occurred in front of Winchester. Not until the evening of the thirteenth did Milroy realize he was facing a portion of the main Confederate army. By then Ewell's Rebels had nearly encircled the town. Fighting became more intense on Sunday, June 14. Jubal Early's Confederate division captured some earthworks near the town and threatened two major Federal fortifications. That evening, Milroy ordered the abandonment of Winchester and the retreat of his troops to Harpers Ferry. The Federals began their retreat shortly after midnight, marching northward along the Martinsburg Pike. The Twelfth Pennsylvania Cavalry was among the advance elements. At Stephenson's Depot the Yankees ran into Confederates from Edward Johnson's division. In a swirling, confused night battle, the Federal force suffered heavy causalities but succeeded in breaking through the Rebel lines. Some Federals escaped to Harpers Ferry. Others, including the surviving part of the Twelfth Cavalry, retreated into southern Pennsylvania.[10]

The Winchester debacle had opened Maryland and Pennsylvania for invasion and had cost the Federals nearly 4,500 men, the great majority missing or captured. The Twelfth Cavalry lost 4 killed, 12 wounded, and 156 missing. Again the unit had not performed particularly well. For the second time in less than a year, the Twelfth had been driven from a battlefield in disorder. A Federal officer at Winchester later testified that the regiment was not "efficient, nor do I believe that they carried out their orders in a great many instances as they should and might have done." General Milroy criticized the regiment's initial reconnaissance, carried out on June 12, and a Milroy aide blamed Captain Morgan of the Twelfth for the loss of a Federal artillery battery. In defense of the unit, however, few Federals at the so-called Second Battle of Winchester would earn praise for their conduct, particularly Milroy himself.[11]

The Twelfth Pennsylvania did not play a significant role during the remainder of Lee's invasion, which would culminate in the decisive Battle of Gettysburg. Following the Winchester defeat, most of the unit assembled at Bloody Run, Pennsylvania, with Colonel Pierce again in command. At McConnellsburg in late June, the regiment skirmished briefly with Confederate forces. On July 4, after the Rebels had begun their retreat from Gettysburg, the Twelfth accomplished its major success of the campaign. At Cunningham Cross Roads, near Greencastle, Pennsylvania, along with a portion of the First New York Cavalry, the Twelfth found a portion of the Confederate army's supply train. More than one hundred wagons were captured by the Federals, along with three cannon, 550 horses and mules, and more than five hundred Rebel soldiers. Near Mercersburg several days later, the regiment captured additional wagons and prisoners. Despite these late successes, the Gettysburg campaign did nothing to improve the reputation of the regiment.[12]

Shortly after the conclusion of the Gettysburg campaign, the Twelfth Cavalry moved to Martinsburg, West Virginia. The regiment would serve in the vicinity of Martinsburg, Charles Town, and Harpers Ferry for most of the remainder of the war.

* * *

Centerville, Pennsylvania
June 16, 1863
Miss Jennie Dear:

I suppose you have heard of the almost or alltogether disastrous battle and defeat of our troops in Winchester on Friday, Saturday, Sunday & Monday. I have the good luck to tell you that I escaped through the heat of the whole affray without a scar on myself or horse.

The battle opened slightly on Friday evening. On Saturday morning it opened in more earnest continued on with success to us all day. At night we closed and were on picket all night. The next morning it opened again very warm and continued with success to us until about 5 o'clock [when] the tune turned against us, and very much too. The rebels opened on us with about 34 pieces of Artillery and fired shell shot & railroad iron until dark when they made a desperate charge with 20,000 Infantry and came near taking our forts. They then surrounded us entirely, with the calculation of taking us all prisoners in the morning.

About 2 o'clock in the morning we left with the intention of cutting through their lines and at daylight we met a large force of them and then & there was opened one of the bloodiest battles on record. It lasted two hours. We could not all get through, the greater part of the cavalry that was [not] killed or wounded made their escape, each one for himself. I and a squad of 30 made our way to Hancock, [but] found no one there to report to. We set out for Baltimore by way of Bedford, we had heard the rebels were in Chambersburg. On arriving at this place 13 miles from Bedford we met General Kelley[13] and reported to him. On tomorrow we leave for Newcreek[14] on the Baltimore & Ohio Railroad. So good by my Love to you & thank God that I am still safe from harm.

> From your true Lover
> John H. Black
> Company G 12. Pa Cav
> Washington D.C.

* * *

Head Qrs. 12. Pa. Cav.
Bedford, Pa.
July 1/63
Dear Jennie:

It is some two weeks since I last wrote to you, and probably you think "Rebs" have taken me, or I have run away entirely. Not so. I am still safe and among the living and healthy. The morning after I wrote to you I left as I told you I would, for Newcreek. On coming within one mile of Cumberland, the "Rebs" threw several shells into the town and shortly after came in themselves. I stood there with my pony and watched them so long as I thought it was healthy. I then turned around and moved to Centerville again. There I remained two days and nights, keeping a strict lookout for the enemy. There were 40 of us together. We then moved on to Bedford, [and] arrived on Friday. On the same day we joined the regiment, moved on to Bloody Run, and from there to McConnellsburg, where we remained for several days, until a strong force of "Rebs" moved on towards the place. Our troops all left the place leaving our company in the rear. We went up the mountain with 14 men and met the "Rebel" advance and had a pretty brisk skirmish with them. Finding they were too many for us, we fell back slowly firing all the while. Sorry to say we had three men wounded in the affray, among which was my highly esteemed friend Sergeant Stiffler.[15] He is now at home on furlough.

We fell back to Bloody Run, and after remaining there for a few days we moved to Bedford on yesterday evening, and purpose remaining here a few days. I am next thing to home. I have put up in town at my Cousin's Adam B. Carns, and am treated very kindly. Oh! how I would wish to get to go home for a few days to see you and the folks at home. Some of our boys did go home and have returned. I might have gone but would not without leave. Probably I may get home in a week or so. If you see me come depend upon it, my Dear Girl that I have leave to go, for if I never get home until I go without leave, you need never expect to see me. I like to go home as well as anyone in the Army, but I have taken an oath to my country and I intend to obey it in every word and letter, through my life should be lost in it.

The Winchester affray was awful as I told you before, and if I ever I get to see you I can tell you more. We lost in our company 28 enlisted men and one Lieutenant.[16] That is they are all missing. They include all killed, wounded, and captured. I was lucky and so escaped unhurt. Poor Sam Evans and William Gwin, with whom you are acquainted are among the missing. What has been their fate I do not know, poor fellows. I would like to know what has become of them. Jacob Walters reported to the Company about a half hour ago. I was very glad to see him. He looks pretty well, but still not really able for hard service.

I saw hosts of the Blair Co. Boys in the Malitia [sic] Companies. James Hammer and I had a great talk together.

My best respects to your mother, aunt and to all others you see fit to remember me to.

So Dear Jennie my undivided Love to you, with the assurance that I feel all right and always think of you wherever I be, So no more but expect to hear from you soon. While I remain your true as ever and ever will be,

> Yours
> John H. Black
> Company "G" 12 Pa. Cav.
> Bedford, Pa.

* * *

12th Pa. Cav.
Head Quarters Co. "G"
Sheppard's Ford, Md.
Potomac River
July 20/63
My true and loving Friend Jennie:

My last to you was from Hagerstown on the 16th Inst. [not in this volume] and on that day we left there at noon and moved on to Sharpsburg where we arrived in the evening. Our company was immediately detailed to go to the above named "Ford" 4 miles form Sharpsburg and it is here we have been doing picket duty ever since on the Maryland shore of the Potomac while the Rebels are at the same duty on the Virginia shore. We are within hailing distance of them and are not allowed to fire at them and they not at us. Picket firing is strictly forbidden. Our boys get in the little boats occasionally and go over to them, unarmed and have a chat and then return, and at times they come over and get their canteens filled with whiskey and go back. No harm done, on either side. You may think it very strange that the rebels are still to be seen on the Potomac, and our large Army of the Potomac over the River at the same time. But be assured our Army did not cross where they did, but chose rather to cross at Harpers Ferry and thereabouts and thereby they got ahead of the rebels and are now between them and Richmond, having a fight about every day or so, taking prisoners on all occasions.[17]

Everything looks favorable on our side, and I hope it may continue on so. For Oh! glad would I be if I could be at home on Christmas day with the knowledge that the war would be over then and I a discharged soldier, and Oh! how well pleased would my friend Jennie be. It is for your sake that I am so over anxious that this war was over, for I well know that you are still discontent and anxiously awaiting the day when peace will be declared once more throughout the length and breath of our land, and I return home with others to our peaceful homes and pleasant firesides. It is scarcely two weeks since I bid you adieu and it appears as long to me as a month did ere I went home. The oftener I go home the worse I hate to leave, and I truly hope and trust that the next time I do go that I may go with the assurance that I need not go back in the Army again.

Yours fully as true
as ever
yours
John H. Black
Co "G" 12. Pa Cav.
Sharpsburg, Md.

* * *

Hd Quarters 12. Pa. Cav.
Martinsburg, Va.
Aug. 12/63
My Dear Jennie;
    . . . [T]he last I wrote to you was on the 5th if I mistake not. The next morning after I went along with a scout of 150, which lasted four days. The first day we marched to Kearneysville, from there to Charlestown, from thence to Berryville, then to the Shenandoah river, where we crossed at Snicker's ford, and put up for the night in the Gap, having traveled 35 miles through the hot rays of the sun. The next morning we started again and went to Leesburg, and then to White's Ford, on the Potomac River, where we crossed over into Maryland and traveled along the river until we came to Point of Rocks, where we encamped for the night having traveled another 35 miles. Then we stayed until the next day at 2 o'clock in the afternoon when we marched to Harpers Ferry and put up for the night, and the next day back to Martinsburg 100 miles altogether.

We met a few rebels, only stragglers. We captured five. Many things connected with the scout I will relate when I see you again. I am well pleased I was along for I saw the hardest "Secesh" part of the country in our travel that I ever saw before.

Dear Jennie the weather is so very warm and the flies so troublesome that I cannot write very much this time so you will have to excuse me. I am well and hope you are the same. . . .

                        Yours
                        John H. Black
                        Co. "G" 12 Pa. Cav.
                        Martinsburg, Va

* * *

Camp of 12. Pa. Cav.
Martinsburg, Va.
August 26/63
Dear Friend Jennie,
    As the weather is nice and cool today, I will spend a few spare moments in writing a letter to you. . . .

Every day brings more joyous news from the different Armies, and great prospects of a speedy close to this "cruel war," and Oh when that comes to pass, what many hearts will be made glad, particularly those who have near & dear friends in the Army, and have the good grace of seeing them return home safe and sound. And if I should be so fortunate as to be one of the number to return to my home, I know that you will be one of the happiest and best pleased girls, in your little town, and I will be rejoiced to see that day, and I hope and trust that it is not far distant. Time alone will tell the result.

Every thing is very quiet about our lines. No rebels near us so far as we can learn. Duty is still very easy and times good, and we enjoy the times exceedingly well, and why shouldn't we do so. I understand Sam O. Evans is in Blair Co. I hope he will, or has probably has, called on you before this. I would like to see him very much for it appears a long time since I last saw him, and parted with him so suddenly and hastily. How do the folks like the Draft by this time.[18] I suppose it will make some of them "chuckle" a little when they behold their names on the list. Jacob & Barney are well and look very well. My best respects to your mother & aunt and next but not least my Devoted and Sincere Love to you my nearest and most confident friend on this wide world. So I sign myself without fear yours forever and ever will be to death.

Yours only
John H. Black
Co "G" 12 Pa Cav,
Martinsburg, Va.

* * *

Confederate activity in the valley increased in October 1863 with Brig. Gen. John D. Imboden's attack on Charles Town. In conjunction with a northward movement of the Army of Northern Virginia from the Rapidan River, Imboden was ordered to advance down the Shenandoah, guarding the left flank of the main Confederate army. At 2:00 a.m. on October 18, Imboden, with a force of about one thousand men, attacked the Federal garrison at Charles Town. The Confederates found the Union troops barricaded in the courthouse, jail, and several other buildings in the center of town. Col. Benjamin L. Simpson of the Ninth Maryland Infantry commanded the Federal force, which consisted of Simpson's regiment and several cavalry companies. Simpson refused to surrender, but after the Confederates fired several artillery rounds, the Federals abandoned their positions and fled "panic-stricken" toward Harpers Ferry. Additional Rebel forces caught the fleeing Yankees on the edge of town and forced more than four hundred to surrender.

Upon hearing of the Confederate attack, Union troops from Harpers Ferry advanced to recapture Charles Town. Imboden evacuated the town and retired toward Berryville, skirmishing with his pursuers. Confederate losses for the action numbered fewer than fifty, while the Federals lost approximately the same number in killed and wounded, and over four hundred captured. John Black and the Twelfth Cavalry were in Harpers Ferry when the attack on Charles Town occurred, although the Pennsylvanians were apparently not engaged in the Union pursuit of Imboden. Black recounted the details of the action in his October 20, 1863, letter to Jennie.

* * *

Camp of 12. Pa. Vol. Cav.
Near Martinsburg, Va.
October 20/63
My Dear Friend Jennie:
     . . . In my last to you I stated to you the rumor then existing in regard to the movement of an Army of the "Rebs" towards this place. The rumor proved to be a fact but not so large a force as was at first represented. There were about 1500 of them. Instead of coming direct here they turned to the right and attacked the 9th Maryland Infantry (six month men) at Charlestown, Va., whipped them and captured about 150. The force from Harpers Ferry moved out after the "rebs" and drove them Helter skelter and captured a host of them. At the same time we had all preparations made for a battle in case they would move in this direction. We had our line of Battle well arranged and would have given them a very hot reception, But luck would have it they did not reach this place. No fears are entertained at present of any force moving towards us.[19]

All is quiet and all things move as heretofore. The Paroled Prisoners are returning to the Regiment pretty rapidly. Some arrive each day, & by the 28th of this month our friend Sam Evans will be here. I then shall remember you to him as requested. I long for the day to arrive when I will greet him in Camp again, and also all the rest of the boys who have been absent since the Winchester Battle. It appears a long time since we were so unceremoniously separated from them on that long to be remembered 15th day of June 1863.

Well Jennie: You ask me one question that I should have acquainted you ere this, had I not neglected it. And that is "what the boys of the Company who have been at home and seen you say about you." All I can say about that is that they all speak very highly of you in every respect & style you a perfect lady in every respect. And I as one am very proud of it. . . . I am also proud of the fact that you have proven so true to me, while many a poor soldier boy left his home & girl near about the same time that I did and long ere this their girls have proven false to them. But Dear Jennie it is myself that has not been served so, and I never have any fears that I will. . . .

Our duty is hard at present still we bear it with all the fortitude of soldiers and never murmur a word about it. . . .

Dear Jennie: As I have given you about all the news in this vicinity worth mentioning I will close with a few words of consolation to you. You are constantly on my mind, And I take all the care of myself possible, for your sake. Never will I do anything that will have any tendency to bring reproach or disgrace on you. As a soldier I make every effort to perform my duty to the best of my ability. And I well know that you act in the same manner in regard to the same. . . . I take the liberty (which I know I am allowed) to sign myself yours and yours alone and will remain until death finally parts us.

> John H. Black
> Co. "G" 12. Pa. Vol. Cavalry
> Martinsburg, Virginia

P.S. All is quiet 11 o'clock at night. J. H. B.

* * *

Camp of 12th Pa. Vol. Cav.
Near Martinsburg, Va.
Oct. 25/63
My Dear Jennie:

. . . Good health is as yet my fortune, and I am getting along admirably well. Duty has been pretty severe for the past 15 days, on account of the great excitement, but that has been lulled to sleep. Now all is quiet and duty will become easier and we have so far enjoyed the excitement and no doubt will enjoy the quietude likewise.

The weather is daily growing colder & old winter is fast coming on. We do not care, for here we are all snugly quartered for the storms & snows, that is if the "rebs" do not come in too large a force and drive us out. We are better situated this fall than ever we have been since in service, and also in better spirits. We have but one more year or so to wild [sic] away and then we will be clear for our term. Many there will gladly welcome the long looked for time when the 12th will have been discharged, and on your account I hope the day may speedily arrive and I be permitted to return safe to my home and there enjoy the pleasure of the company of my own dear friend. . . .

> Yours
> John H. Black
> Co. "G" 12 Pa. Vol. Cav
> Martinsburg, Va.

* * *

Camp of 12. Pa. Vol. Cav.
Near Martinsburg, Va.
November 2/63
Dear Jennie:

. . . Stirring times with us for a few days past, and not in the least agreeable. It so happened that on or about Thursday last the Colonel Commanding the Forces at this place was sent on detached duty to the city of Washington, and consequently another of the same rank took command, & In order to distinguish himself, or rather let us know that he was vested in authority, He issued an order that our Camp should be moved to the other side of the town from where we then were.[20] Said order had to be obeyed but not in good humor. We left our good and comfortable log building and now have our tents pitched on the ground instead of logs as before. Nevertheless in a few days more we will have our quarters fixed in the same as in last Camp and be ready for another move should somebody else assume the command and make a show of himself.

I received a letter from Skyles today. He states that he is getting along finely. He had been on the sick list a few days, but is now well. He says he received a letter from Lue, but did not say anything about it. Evans has returned to the Company. He looks very well. I was greatly rejoiced to see him. Jacob Walters, Barney & Gwin wish to be remembered to you. . . .

My undivided Love to you while I sigh myself your ever true friend and yours alone,

John H. Black
Co. "G" 12. Pa. Vol. Cav.
Martinsburg, Virginia

* * *

Camp of 12. Pa. Vol. Cavalry
Martinsburg, Va.
Nov. 17/63
My Dear & much Loved Jennie:

. . . I am happy to learn that your health is good, but really sorry to learn that you are so much troubled with that abominable thing the "toothache." I do really pity you my Dear and my sincere and candid advice to you would be to have the *unruly tooth* drawn, and then you would not be troubled so much with it. I think Dear Jennie, that if I could happen to call on you sometime when that tooth troubles you so much & spend a night or so in that *good old rocking chair* of *ours* that this toothache would suddenly leave you. Don't you think so! But what is the use of me talking about that for it will be chance work I do happen to get leave of absence this winter. Nevertheless do not despair & I will not. I intend to do my best to get away long enough to give you a few nights of the old fashioned squeezing, and if I fail to get off, depend upon it, I will not be to blame for I am ever ready to go whenever opportunity affords.

But you are well aware that I am one who will always obey my superior officers, and therefore I will never go home without the legal & proper authority, and then I can go without fear or favor. As I often before told you that my solemn oath to my country must & shall be fulfilled, and thereby cast neither shame nor disgrace on you, myself or relatives. I can conscientiously report myself to you this evening as being in excellent health, as much so as ever I enjoyed.

Everything is quiet and moving along briskly & we are enjoying ourselves in our really comfortable winter quarters in this Camp. The boys of the Company are all in good health and getting along finely. The Company at present numbers 68 men. You had better think we [are] getting along finely when all that number are healthy. . . .

Take all news and reports calm and cool, be as content as nature will allow, and do not trouble yourself too much. Pass the time swiftly by, and enjoy yourself as well as you can. . . .

While I affix my name with the assurance that I am yours & yours only.

John H. Black
Co. "G" 12. Pa. Vol. Cavalry
Martinsburg, Virginia

* * *

Camp 12. Pa. Vol. Cav.
Martinsburg, Va.
December 13/63
My ever Dear & Much Loved Jennie:

Again have I the honor of acknowledging the receipt of two very welcome & neatly written letters, which were read with great respect and interest. Also with the letters was the package containing those *wristbelts*. Jennie I was very well pleased to receive them and to you I return my sincere thanks for the same. I shall wear them in honor of you. They are just the thing that I wished. I am proud to know that you are so very willing to comply with my requests. . . .

I can report myself as heretofore in regard to health. The God above has so far favored me very highly in that respect. I am truly thankful that it has been so. Health is very essential to a soldier. Oh! how I do pity the poor soldiers who have lost their health in the service of their country. To visit any of the government's hospitals, and there see the poor suffering soldiers, in all stages & kind of disease, is enough to melt the hardest heart. And this we say of the soldiers in our own hospitals. How awful must it be, in those Southern prisons, where our poor soldiers are confined as Prisoners of War, with scarcely enough to eat to keep them alive, and in fact many do actually starve to death. Who would have thought ere this cruel war, that any American citizen could ever become so utterly lost and degraded as to allow their fellow beings to starve, while it lay in their power to render aid. God forbid that it should be ever my lot to again fall into the hands of those inhuman and degraded wretches. Wretches I call them. Nay! They are *worse* than wretches. Rather call them *fiends* & *devils* in the *shape* of *men*.

You tell me your Protracted Meeting[21] is over. I don't think you folks are as good christians as the people of this place, for the Protracted here has been going on at a lively rate for some time past and by present appearance, bids fair to continue for weeks to come. Probably it may be that Soldiers are harder to convert than any other class, and for their sakes continue the meeting. Quite a good idea I presume if it be so. Today our *"pious"* Chaplain[22] made his appearance in Camp, called the boys together, in front of the Commanders tent, and preached a short sermon to them in general. What effect it had I do not know, and dare not judge. I think so little of the Chaplain, that it would be very painful to me to listen to him for half hour. I don't think I could endure it at all. I Love to listen to a minister, when he is a man that I can respect, but such a *thing* as we have, had better be somewhere else attending to some other business more appropriate to his *character,* than be preaching to soldiers who *know* him so well as we do. I should not talk so much about a Chaplain but indeed Jennie, I believe that I am saying nothing but what is actually so, in every particular.[23]

We are still at the same place as you can see by the first part of this letter, and will no doubt remain here during the winter and probably longer. All is quiet and nothing of any importance transpiring. Some 4 days ago a large scout of Infantry & Artillery started up the Valley on 15 days scout. I presume they will see something before they return. If they do I will acquaint you of the facts. What object they have in view, is yet to be told. . . .

So you say you would Love to see me come home this winter. I don't doubt you would in the least. And so far as I know you will see me some time this winter. I cannot tell exactly when. Just rest easy as you can and I will be about some time depend upon it. If I don't it will be awful strange indeed.

I would like very well on this (Sunday) evening, instead of writing to you to be with you in the little parlor, having one of our old fashioned talks and times, together as in days past. Never mind I think the day not so very far distant when I will be about. This war cannot last so might long any more, and if it does, why I have not one year more to serve, until my three years will expire & then my mind tells me, I will be quitting a soldier's life, and return to my native county and my friends. . . .

My sincere undivided and ever true Love to you my own Dear friend Jennie.

John H. Black
Co. "G" 12. Pa. Vol. Cav
Martinsburg, Virginia

* * *

Camp 12. Pa. Vol. Cavalry
Martinsburg, Va
December 28/63
My Dear Friend Jennie:

    . . . Discontent is still the ruling Power of you, and all account of one being absent from you. Never mind the time is rolling swiftly by. The three years will soon be past. The 10th of next December, will be the last of the enlistment. If I live I will then return to you, if not sooner. So rest easy my devoted, true, faithful & Loving Girl, and you will meet your friend.

    We are having gay times. Duty very easy & we enjoy the times to perfection. The weather is pleasant as December can be. The year is passing, yes is nearly passed. This will no doubt be the last letter I write to you in the year /63, and then we will see the Leap Year appear. The year that the ladies claim as their own. Ere that year passes by I expect to be with you again, and that to remain with you. You may expect, (as I have told you before) to see me at home this winter, what time I can not say at all.

    The Revival is still going on as lively as ever. Many souls are saved, at least professed to be. I have not been to a meeting yet. The boys nearly all attend. . . .

            With my name as yours
            & yours alone
            John H. Black

Lt. John H. Black, Twelfth Pennsylvania Volunteer Cavalry.

John H. Black later in life.

Black and his wife, Jennie, and their children.

Chapter 4

1864

The year 1864 would bring an increase in major military operations in the Shenandoah Valley. Confederate leaders realized that the lower valley must be given primary attention since it remained the gateway to the Union capital, while the Federal command sought to deny the South this traditional invasion route.

Despite repeated letters to Jennie expressing his desire to leave the army and come home, Black agreed to serve beyond his initial contract, apparently thinking that if he reenlisted as an officer he could resign anytime. Yet given his dedication to the cause, it was not uncommon for soldiers to remain in the service against their desires to return home to their loved ones.[1] The winter of 1863–64 passed relatively quietly for the Twelfth Cavalry. The Pennsylvanians comprised a part of the Union forces of the Department of West Virginia, commanded by Brig. Gen. Benjamin F. Kelley. As part of Col. Robert S. Rodgers's Third Brigade in Brig. Gen. Jeremiah Sullivan's First Division, the regiment guarded the Baltimore and Ohio Railroad in the vicinity of Martinsburg for most of this period. The regiment, "with the exception of an occasional collision with the Rebel cavalry and bushwhackers, . . . remained employed in the usual guard, scout, and picket duty, without serious molestation, until the opening of the campaign of 1864."[2]

On the last day of 1863 and the first day of the new year, John Black and a detachment of the Twelfth Cavalry participated in a scout toward Bunker Hill. On January 1 a portion of the Federal force moved out in the direction of Winchester. En route they skirmished with a small group of Confederates, capturing several. The Federals were then surprised by a larger force and retreated back to Bunker Hill and, eventually, Martinsburg.

The affair at Bunker Hill caused much consternation and anger among the Federal command. Initial reports from the pickets indicated that a brigade of Confederates was advancing on Martinsburg. These exaggerated claims proved false. Brigadier General Cutler, whose troops guarded the B&O, reported on the evening of January 1 that "a scare of the pickets was magnified to a great extent, since the heavy firing reported [by the pickets] on Tuscarora road turns out to be a salute for the new year." Gen. William Averell added that he did not have "much confidence in the [reports of the] pickets of the Twelfth Pennsylvania," an assertion with which Brigadier General Kelley concurred.[3]

From Second Bull Run in 1862 through to this 1864 New Year's Day skirmish, the hard luck Twelfth Pennsylvania had consistently failed to perform even to the most modest expectations. Undoubtedly John Black and his companions hoped that the new year would bring more successful results.

* * *

Camp 12. Pa. Vol. Cavalry
Martinsburg, Va.
January 3/64
My Dear Friend Jennie:
New Year's day has come and past & the year in full blast and at the same time intensely cold all the while thus far. Oh! but it is cold, colder than any weather I have experienced since I have been soldiering. Do not be the least alarmed when I tell you how I commenced this year. On the 30th of last month, the news reached us that a considerable force of

"rebs" was seen in the *Valley* and intended to visit this place & pay us in return for what a portion of our Department did under General Averill[4] a few weeks ago. We have kept scouting parties out all the time since, with the intention of watching their movements and be ready for them. In the meantime General Averill moved his forces to this place to assist us in case of an attack and give them a warm reception, with a few of Uncle Sam's well-made Pills.

The evening of the 31st a scout of 30 men (among which number I was) went to Bunker Hill (10) miles from here, and lay there on Picket for the night. At 2 o'clock on New Year's morning a Lieutenant & (7) men, of our number moved on in the direction of Winchester. After having traveled about 7 or 8 miles, they were halted by some "rebs" who were doing Picket. This little squad of our boys charged upon them & captured 5 of them. Our boys then turned back, thinking they had done well enough, and gone as far as they thought safe for that time. They traveled along in good glee for several miles, when all at once a squad of about 30 "rebs" charged out of a thick wood on to our gallant little squad, which had to do the best they could. The prisoners were recaptured & sorry to say that they captured Sergt. Stiffler of Co. "G" as good a soldier as ever drew a saber.[5] The others escaped and joined us again at Bunker Hill. We immediately gave chase but could not over take them, & so my much esteemed friend Stiffler is a Prisoner of War and will have to endure the suffering and hardship on that "Belle Isle"[6] where many a poor soldier had breathed his last. I pity the man that is taken these times. I still hope that an arrangement will soon be made, and then a good one, to have all Prisoners exchanged.

We spent the New Year's day at Bunker Hill and at night returned to Camp. The rumor is still afloat that the "rebs" have a large force at or near Winchester. We have a scout of 100 men out at present from our Regiment, who had quite a brisk Skirmish with them this morning. If they intend taking this place they had better bring more force than they have at Winchester. I have no idea that they will come down here to bother us at all. The report just came in that the "rebs" are falling back. All will be quiet in a few days.

On my return from that scout I received two very interesting and loving letters and will answer them both in this. I was happy to learn of your good health and in return I can say that my health is excellent & I am at all times ready & willing to do my duty as a soldier, and will do so if health & life permits until the 10th of December, 1864, and then I will quit soldiering and not reenlist, but return to my native County and State, and let others reenlist who think proper. If it were not for you I would have reenlisted before this. It is for your sake alone that I will forsake a soldier's life at the expiration of my three years. So much I love you, you have often told me in your letters to not reenlist. And now my Dear Jennie, the loved one to me of this wide world, I will solemnly make this candid vow to you. That if God spares my life until the expiration of my term I will return to you. So rest easy, if others do reenlist, you can safely say that there is one in the Army that loves you so dearly that for your sake he will not reenlist.

Remember what I have said on this page is what I really mean. . . .

Sam O. Evans will leave for Penna. in a few days. He will call to see you.

> My love to you as I close
> My name to this as your and
> yours alone.
> John H. Black

* * *

Reenlistment, Marriage, and Promotion

John Black often spoke to Jennie of the fact that he would not remain in the service after the expiration of his unit's term of service. The men of the Twelfth had enlisted in late 1861 and early 1862 for three years, making them eligible for discharge in late 1864 and early 1865. Many other veteran regiments were to be discharged in the spring and summer of 1864, a fact that worried the Union high command greatly.

With Lt. Gen. Ulysses Grant now in Washington to person-ally direct the spring campaign against Lee, a strong effort was made over the winter of 1863–64 to encourage men to extend their enlistments. Benefits to those who reenlisted included a sub-stantial bounty and furlough and the right to be called a "Veteran Volunteer." Additionally, if the required percentage of a unit re-enlisted, the unit would remain in service and not be disbanded. If this percentage was not reached, the Veteran Volunteers would be sent to new units and the old regiment broken up.

The Twelfth Pennsylvania was not disbanded, as John Black and the majority of his comrades reenlisted. Loyalty to their unit and their country certainly affected many, although the bounty and furlough induced more than a few to stay in the service. Black reenlisted on February 1, 1864. Ironically, as recently as January 3 he had assured Jennie he would not reenlist. At some point, apparently in late February or early March, he left his unit for a furlough home. Black took the opportunity of his visit to marry his longtime love. He and Jennie exchanged vows on April 3, 1864.

There is gap in the Black letters from January 3 through April 26. During part of the period Black was home on furlough. The exact dates of Black's furlough are unclear, as is his itinerary. Black apparently did some recruiting for his unit while in Pennsylvania. In his letter of April 26, 1864, he mentions being at the Chester, Pennsylvania, army hospital. It is not believed however, that Black was a patient in the hospital at this time. He probably was simply visiting a friend or stopping at Chester on his journey back to his unit.

At about the time of his return to Virginia, Black also was promoted from first sergeant in Company G to second lieutenant. His promotion orders, signed by the commander of the Department of West Virginia, Franz Sigel, were dated April 28, 1864. Black now had both a new wife and new title. For the rest of 1864 the Twelfth served around Harpers Ferry and Charles Town, scouting the area for Rebels.[7]

* * *

Camp Davis
Near Sandy Hook, Md.
April 26, 1864
My Dear Jennie:

Once again will I make the attempt to pen you a few lines for no doubt you will anxiously be looking for another letter from me. I wrote to you on the 20th while we were at Chester Hospital telling you not to answer until I wrote again, which will be this. We remained at the Hospital until Saturday noon, at which time we took the train and landed at Baltimore in the evening; there we remained at all night. The next morning we got aboard the train again, and by evening we landed at *Sandy Hook*, one mile from Harpers Ferry. There we passed the night in the cars. Next morning (being yesterday) (Monday) we set out a foot for the above named Camp which we found after traveling 4 miles.

Here we are to remain until we all get horses which may be in a few weeks and on the other hand, may not be for months to come. All right with me, I can content myself as well here as any other place. Wherever I go I make myself at home, that is my nature you know, but still my homes are not all alike as you well know. I am in excellent health and have been so since I left home. Excuse another short [letter] as accommodations for writing are very poor. . . .

Enclosed you will find my picture, which you will please hand over to Mollie Slayman with my best wishes (one picture for yourself). . . .

My ever true Love to you while to this I attach my name as your affectionate and ever devoted Husband.

> John H. Black
> Co. "G" 12. Pa. V. Cavalry
> Camp Davis
> Near Sandy Hook, Maryland
> The next letter I will do better

* * *

Bolivar Heights, Va.
May 6, 1864
My Dear Jennie:

Again will write to you in order to fulfill my promise to write at least once every week. This is the fourth letter to you since I left home and up till this day at noon I have not received any from you. But that is easily accounted for, when I last wrote I was in Camp Davis, Md. Since that time some of us have received horses and are at the above named place doing duty. Duty we have here is easy, nothing but picketing & drilling. That is we drill the new recruits. Our Company now numbers 104 men. When all are out it makes a grand appearance. This is a very warm day. I am sitting in the Sunshine writing away and do not mind the heat. We will have our tent rigged up a little by tomorrow and then we can get along in the shade. No "Rebs" about here, General Sigel's force is at Winchester. . . .

Jennie, I have parted with you six times all together, but the last time was the hardest to bear. I though it could hardly be that I was to leave you after being married, but you know duty called me away, and it had to be done. Often do I sit & think of you and wonder how you are getting along, for I know you are still as discontented as ever. I Pity you indeed I do from the bottom of my heart, for I know you are my best &

dearest friend on this earth and ever will remain so. Oh! If I only were as certain of returning home to you as I am that you will ever prove true to me, would I not feel good. The more I sit & think about you the more firmly I become attached to you, & with all we have to be separated for awhile yet I hope it may not be long anymore.

Sam O. Evans is in the Quarter Master Department in Camp Davis, Md. & probably will remain there all summer. Jacob Walters & Barney Engle are both well. The weather is very warm. We have a pleasant Camp.

Well dear Jennie I have at last got the uniform on and doing duty differently from what I had at before. . . .

We left Joe. Lundy[8] in the Hospital at Camp Davis. He can't stand soldiering at all. . . .

My ever true undivided & devoted Love to you while to this my name

as your affectionate Husband
Lieut. John H. Black
Co. "G" 12. Pa. V. Cav.
Harpers Ferry, Virginia

* * *

Bolivar Heights, Va,
Sunday, May 8, 1864
My Dear Jennie:

This forenoon while I was sitting alone in my Shelter tent I had the satisfaction & pleasure of having a letter from you, handed to me. . . .

I trust this war will soon end and I be permitted to return home safe to you, where we (God permitting) will spend many happy days together. I am well and getting along finely. Have not much to do. Our duty consists of Picketing & drilling the new recruits. I do love to drill the men in Co. "G." They are all so obedient and very willing to learn. It is a pleasure to be among such men.

This is a very pleasant & healthy place. We have very little sickness in our Camp. I have not heard from Otto & Molly since I left home, & indeed from no other person but yourself. I cannot imagine what becomes of the mail. I suppose some of these days I will get a whole pack of letters in one day. . . .

Jacob Walters, Barney Engle & Sam O. Evans are well and wish to be remembered to you with respect. Sam has got right well again since he has got to Camp again. . . .

My ever true & undivided Love to you. While to this my name

> as your true & devoted &
> affectionate
> Husband
> Lieut. John H. Black
> Co. "G" 12. Pa. V Cavalry
> Harpers Ferry, Virginia

* * *

Camp 12th Pa. Vol. Cavalry
Bolivar Heights, Va.
June 3, 1864
My Dear & Much Loved Wife:

. . . My only wish and heart's desire is that this war may speedily come to an end and thereby permit me to return to you safe & sound, and with you in peace spend many happy years, for such a life we will undoubtedly lead if ever we are by kind Providence, permitted to meet after the close of this wicked Rebellion. . . .

Your inquiry about Sergt. William Stiffler of our Company can be answered by telling you that to the best of my knowledge (and sorry to say it) he is still in the hands of the "rebels." In March last he was sent from Richmond to the State of Georgia. Poor Billy he must have endured many hardships and privations and is still doing so yet. I could shed tears for him, if it would do him a particle of good. . . .

> Your true, affectionate &
> ever devoted
> Husband
> Lieut. John H. Black
> Co. "G" 12. Pa. V. Cavalry
> Harpers Ferry, Virginia

* * *

Camp 12th Pa. V. Cavalry
Camp Bolivar Heights, Va.
June 10, 1864
My ever Dear & Loving Wife:

. . . This has been quite a cool day, it reminded one of a pleasant Autumn day, more so at least than Summer, with all that a very interesting and loving letter from you was highly welcome and cheerfully greeted by the writer of this. . . .

I have volunteered to defend my country's cause and am doing so cheerfully & so far as I know, obediently. Quite a consolation is it still to me to hear from you so regularly, and at every time to receive the glad & welcome tidings that you are the possessor of excellent health. . . .

Queer indeed to me, is how people can manufacture so much news about our Regiment as to have it rumored that we are in front of Richmond. True, if we were ordered to the front, we would go obediently and do our duty, But up to the present time we have not received any orders to leave here.

On yesterday a scout of 60 men of our Regt. were on a scouting tour, across the Shenandoah River in Loudoun Co., Va., came in contact with a rebel scouting party. After quite a brisk & lively skirmish of a half an hour our boys drove them, succeeding in capturing one Lieutenant & 8 men. We lost not a man, in killed wounded, or prisoner. I was on duty in Camp and consequently was not detailed to go along. . . .[9]

It was quite a surprize to me to hear that John W. Hicks[10] resigned, particularly [in] as such times as these. But I presume he had his reasons for doing so, better known to him than us. I noticed in the County Papers that there is a Samuel Black[11] on the list of drafted men. Do you know whether it is Brother Samuel? I would like very much to know, I have not heard from any of them since two weeks past.

You appear to be the only regular correspondent I have. The others all appear to be very tardy. What has become of Mollie & [H]erman?[12] I have not heard much about them of late. I suppose they are enjoying the honey-moon, and do not trouble their minds much about any other person. Luck to them all the time say I.

I am sorry to hear that John Laise[13] is so badly wounded. I think that if his father had any fatherly feeling for him, he would go to see him & try to get him home.

Every thing is moving cheerfully & smoothly in this section. Our duty is as easy as ever, And we are enjoying it cheerfully. Joseph E. Engle[14] reported to the company yesterday evening, he looks as well as ever. There are at present but three of our Company absent, two of which, (Stiffler and Gardner)[15] are prisoners and in the Hospital in Maryland. There is but one in the Hospital at this place, and that is *Joseph Lundy.* I fear he will never get out of that, Poor fellow I pity him very much. The others 101 are all in Camp & well. Barney, Evans & Walters are well & wish to [be] remembered with great respect to you. . . .

Jennie Dear, To you I say, be as content as nature will allow, take good care of yourself. Let time glide by as swiftly as possible, trusting that you & I will live to see the end of this wicked rebellion [and] be permitted to meet each other again knowing that peace is once more restored to our country and then live together in peace & harmony for years to come. Such is my prayer & I know it is yours too from the heart.

My Dear Wife to you my ever Devoted & undivided Love now & forever & ever.

While to this I cheerfully attach my name as your true, Devoted & Affectionate Husband.

Lieut. John H. Black
Co. "G" 12. Pa. V. Cavalry
Harpers Ferry, Virginia

To
Jennie Black
Duncanville
Blair Co. Pa.

* * *

In the summer and fall of 1864, the Shenandoah Valley became the scene of heavy fighting. Gen. Jubal Early was detached from Gen. Robert E. Lee's Army of Northern Virginia from the lines around Petersburg to operate in the valley. Lee hoped to draw Federal troops away from Petersburg and preserve Confederate control over the Shenandoah. After initial Confederate successes, including a threatening move against Washington, D.C., Lt. Gen. Ulysses S. Grant ordered Maj. Gen. Philip Sheridan to take command of Union forces in the valley and drive Early out. In a masterful campaign, Sheridan would rout Early and lay waste to the Confederate breadbasket.

John Black and the Twelfth Cavalry would be heavily involved in the subsequent campaign. In early to mid-July, the regiment, now part of the First Brigade of the First Cavalry Division, participated in actions at Solomon's Gap, Pleasant Valley, and Crampton's Gap. At Pleasant Valley the Pennsylvanians were commended for their "gallantry" by their brigade commander.

The Twelfth also was heavily engaged at the July 23–24 Battle of Kernstown, where Early's forces attacked Union troops under the command of Maj. Gen. George Crook. On the twenty-third the regiment fought dismounted as skirmishers and assisted in driving back the Confederate defenders. On the following day, however, the reinforced Confederates forced the Federals to retreat with heavy casualties. Col. William B. Tibbits's cavalry brigade, including the Twelfth, charged the enemy at the battle's close and checked their pursuit. The Pennsylvanians suffered one killed and nineteen wounded in the battle. Colonel Tibbits commended Lieutenant Colonel Bell of the Twelfth and Lieutenant Colonel Augustus Root of the Fifteenth New York Cavalry "for the brave and efficient manner in which they commanded their regiments, especially when their commands were dismounted on the skirmish line."[16]

* * *

Bolivar Heights, Va.
Aug. 7/64
My Dear & Much Loved Wife:
. . . Oh! But I would love to be with you this day. God only knows when I will get to see you. I trust it will not be long. I suppose the people are on a great scare[17] again in Pennsylvania, about the *rebels*. If they would have seen and met as many as we have since the 4th of July they would get used to seeing them. On the 4th of this month we had quite a lively and spirited skirmish with the chaps about 8 miles from [here]. It lasted for two hours. We had two men wounded, 5 horses wounded & 3 horses killed. We brought all the men off the battlefield. It was one of the most brilliant skirmishes that I have been in during the war. I and my horse escaped unhurt. The whole affair was grand victory on our part.[18] Today everything is quiet in this section. Quite a large Army moved through here on yesterday and the day before. They will find the enemy this evening or tomorrow.

Dear Jennie: I am very sorry to report to you that I lost that picture of yours. I never was so sorry for anything in my life before, but so it is. I cannot help, I thought I was taking all the care of it I could. I trust you will soon send me that Photograph you spoke of and also send one to your cousin (Maggie Black, Smicksburg, Indiana Co., Pa). . . .[19]

Jennie How are the folks at the Toll gate[20] by this time. I suppose they rejoiced when the news was afloat that I was killed or badly wounded, but disappointed no doubt when they found that it was a false rumor. I do not know how such news gets afloat. I suppose some chap has been writing that I was wounded on the 4th of July and did not state how badly and from that rumor arose. If no one gets worse wounded than I have been they need not fear. For my part I did not call it a wound. It was only a scratch as the ball passed by. Jennie rest easy, it is my opinion that I am to live to see the end of this wicked rebellion and return to you and live for years to come in harmony and happiness.

Barney Engle, Will Gwin, Evans are well and also is Joe. Lundy. . . .

Your true, devoted & affectionate
Husband
Lieut. John H. Black
Co. "G" 12. P. V. Cav.
Harpers Ferry, Va.

* * *

On August 21, 1864, the Twelfth participated in another vigorously fought battle, known as Cameron's Depot (Welch's Spring), located west of Charles Town near Summit Point. In this engagement Jubal Early's Confederates surprised a portion of Sheridan's troops and, after sharp fighting, succeeded in driving the Yankees back through Charles Town and east toward Halltown. The Federals suffered 260 casualties in the battle, and the Confederates lost fewer than 50. Despite the defeat, the Twelfth Cavalry seems to have performed well, erasing to a degree their less-successful operations of 1862 and 1863.[21]

* * *

Bolivar Heights, Va.
Aug. 22/64
My Dear Wife Jennie:

. . . I suppose you have great rumors in regard to the Army of the Shenandoah. Times are very lively and interesting. The Grand Ball opened at daylight yesterday morning about 4 mile from Charlestown and was kept up pretty brisk all day. It opened again this morning and while I write I hear the cannon booming quite lively. The Cavalry had very heavy fighting yesterday. Our regiment the *gallant 12th* made a bold and daring charge through the enemy's line yesterday afternoon and charged back again, but sad was the fate of many of the boys. Lieut. Col. Bell[22] & the Adjutant[23] were both wounded and are now in town. Quite a number were killed & wounded. We lost heavily in horses. No one need to charge the 12th with cowardice any more. She went on the charge yesterday after two other Regiments refused. I did not happen to be with it. I was ordered to the Regiment on the 19th of this month and on the 20th I was ordered back to this place again, and will remain here for some time to come. I cannot give you much news in regards to the battle that is now raging,[24] but will when I write again if I am spared do so. Barney Engle has returned to us again, he had been taken prisoner the day we went to Martinsburg, but escaped since. Was he not lucky. He is well and feels lively after getting away from the rebels. Sam. Evans, Gwin & Lundy are living and well. . . .

My ever true & undivided Love to you while tis this my name as your True devoted &

> Affectionate
> Husband
> Lieut. John H. Black
> Co. "G" 12. P. V. Cav
> Harpers Ferry, Virginia

* * *

Camp 12. Pa. V. Cav.
Bolivar Heights, Va.
Oct. 2/64
My Dear Wife:

. . . I was pleased to learn that you are still in excellent health and getting along finely. I in return can inform [you] that I have a very severe cold, otherwise well enough. The cold will soon disappear. I had a letter from home a few days ago. Jerry made mention of you being there, I was pleased to hear it, indeed I was. I wish I could have been there with you, But I could not & so it is. You appear to be very anxious to see me, no doubt of it [at] all, and I would much like to see you, but at present it can not be, but in all probability it will be sometime [in] the coming winter, providing I am living and not in the hands of the rebels.

The rebs are pretty scarce in the Valley these times. Sheridan has whipped them shamefully and driven (what he did not kill or catch) over one hundred miles and still in pursuit of them yet. He is the General for this Valley.[25] A few more such whippings to the rebels will end this war and let us soldiers go home. I think the end of the war is fast coming. It cannot come too soon for me, provided it is ended honorably. No other

way do I ever wish to see it ended. Oh! When this war is [over] all soldiers
be permitted to return home safe to those whom the[y] love. . . .
Everything is quiet about here and now. . . .

> Your ever true devoted &
> Affectionate
> Husband
> Lieut. John H. Black
> Co. "G" 12. Pa. V. Cav.
> Harpers Ferry, Va

* * *

Camp 12th Pa. V. Cav.
Bolivar Heights, Va.
Oct. 4, 1864
My Dear Wife:
. . . It is my privilege this evening to report to you in the best of
health. My headache & bad cold have disappeared and left me again
perfectly well. I am very thankful that such is the case.

I was very pleased to hear that you spent a few days at Father's.
I trust you had a gay and joyous time, and spent the time agreeably. I
always love to hear of you being out at home. If I am so situated that I
cannot go with you out there I am glad that you can go. I trust that the
time will soon come that I will be permitted to go with you. . . .

Times are gay in the Valley. No enemy near at present except a few
Guerrillas occasionally and they do not amount to anything, Sheridan is
over 100 miles from here, and did very well. He is one of those Generals
that gains victories & follows them up. I see by the papers that Grant[26]
is moving bold & surely on toward Richmond. I don't think the day far
distant until the news will be sent forth on the wires that Petersburg &
Richmond are ours. Oh! What Glorious news that will be. The day is
fast drawing night when this war will be over at least I have that opinion. And then the soldiers [will] be permitted to return to their beloved
homes. Me to my Dear Wife never more to leave her while life remains.
Oh! Will not that be joyful news to you & me. I wish that day were here
and I know you do too. We will have to wait.

Sam O. Evans, Gwin & Barney are with us yet & well, Lundy went
home on Furlough (sick) some ten days ago. He promised to write to me,
but has not yet done it. He did not say whether he would call to see you,
I trust he will. . . .

Your ever true, devoted &
Affectionate
Husband
Lieut. John H. Black
Co. "G" 12 Pa. V. Cav.
Harpers Ferry, Va.

* * *

Col. John Mosby's Confederate partisans became even more active during the fall of 1864. Perhaps Mosby's most famous and daring exploit was the so-called Greenback Raid of October 13–14, 1864. After learning that Federal paymasters had left Washington on the Baltimore and Ohio tracks, Mosby set out across the Shenandoah River on the night of the thirteenth to raid the train carrying the paymasters. When they arrived at Duffield's Depot, twenty men were assigned to the task of pulling up the rails. On completion of the job, the men hid in the bushes and waited for the approaching train, which to their surprise passed right by. The Baltimore and Ohio Railroad was double tracked through Jefferson County and the men had torn up the wrong track. Infuriated by their blunder, Mosby ordered the men to tear up the other track and decided to wait for the next train. Although Mosby did not realize it at the time, the two paymasters had missed their train and had to take the next express. At 2:15 a.m. on the fourteenth, the next train approached, and after a great rumble it derailed. Mosby's men boarded the train and robbed the paymasters and found some $168,000 in greenbacks. Mosby then ordered the train burned and fled the scene, returning safely across the Shenandoah River. John Black would leave a vivid account of the raid and of the Federals' efforts to capture Mosby.[27]

* * *

Camp 12 Pa. V. Cav.
Bolivar Heights, Va.
Sunday, Oct. 16/64
My Dear Wife:
    . . . The weather is very pleasant, just cool enough. These cool nights are splendid for sleeping. Mosquitoes & gnats do not gnaw at a person

when asleep. Winter is drawing near, just the time I enjoy soldiering when in good health. Through the kindness of an all wise Providence I am permitted to report myself in excellent health and able for any military duty imposed on me. Duty is pretty easy with us at present. How long it will continue so I cannot tell. The health of the Regiment is getting better, [with] very few sick. Two weeks ago we had quite a large sick list but the Doctor has cured nearly all of them.

Everything is quiet in the Valley. There was quite an excitement here the other morning. A Squad of Mosby's Guerilla's made their appearance on the Baltimore & Ohio Railroad about 7 miles from here in the direction of Martinsburg. [They] run the Express train off the track, captured all the passengers aboard, making prisoners of all the soldiers whom they robbed of all their money, jewelry, and in fact everything that was of any value. Among them was a Paymaster from whom they took seventy thousand dollars. The citizens and women the[y] robbed of all their money, hats, shoes, coats, jewelry, shawls and all that to them proved valuable. They then set fire to the train (after taking out the baggage & express safe) and burnt it, leaving therein a corpse of a poor soldier that was being sent home to his friends, inhuman wretches. When this was completed they mounted speedily, released the citizens & ladies, and made their way to Snicker's Ferry with all possible speed & were soon safe in the mountains. As soon as the news reached Harpers Ferry all the available force was sent in pursuit of the marauders. We went as fast as the horses could carry us, but they had made their time good and were gone. They will come once too often. If we get hold of that crew, remember we will deal none too easy with them. The road is all right again as though nothing had happened. The damage done the Railroad Company in burning the train is about twelve thousand dollars.

We are busily engaged in drilling new recruits. We have filled our Regiment again to replace the loss of this Summer, But those last men we received are all one year chaps. By the time they get properly initiated into the realities of a soldiers duty & life their time will expire, and I trust the war will be over ere that time and we all can get home. . . .

Your true devoted & affectionate Husband

Lieut. John H. Black

Co. "G" 12. Pa. V. Cav.

Harpers Ferry, Virginia

* * *

The last major battle of the 1864 Valley campaign occurred on October 19, 1864, at Cedar Creek. Jubal Early's Confederates nearly drove the Federal force from the field and won a major victory. Philip Sheridan, however, arrived on the field after his immortal ride and assisted in rallying his men. Although Cedar Creek ended major fighting in the Shenandoah, smaller ambushes, raids, and skirmishes would continue until the end of the war. The guerrilla warfare fought in this area of Virginia was vastly different from the conventional fighting taking place before Petersburg. It required aggressive, self-reliant leadership at the regimental level, along with seasoned veterans conditioned to perform independently. A majority of the officers and men of the Twelfth Pennsylvania Cavalry did not seem to possess these traits. Constant changes in the command structure did little to foster unit cohesion, and the Second Manassas and Winchester debacles severely damaged the Twelfth's esprit de corps. The regiment also seemed to suffer from a chronic shortage of men, equipment, and, particularly, horses.

In an October 1864 letter to Maj. Gen. Philip Sheridan, Brig. Gen. John D. Stevenson, commanding the Military District of Harpers Ferry, was extremely critical of the Twelfth. He called the unit "not strictly reliable," adding that as "a Cavalry, it was a farce to give me the Twelfth Pennsylvania and call it a cavalry. They have only 336 men, ostensibly mounted, of which number not more than 200 can turn out mounted for the field."[28]

General Sheridan soon gained his own negative impression of the Twelfth. Following continued attacks by Mosby's men in the valley and the seeming inability of Union forces to eradicate the guerrillas, Sheridan wrote in exasperation to Stevenson. "It is reported that Major Congdon, of the Twelfth Pennsylvania, reports the enemy in force at or near Charles Town," he fumed, and he ordered him to "find out if he has made this untruthful report." "If the Twelfth Pennsylvania cavalry cannot keep that country clear of guerrillas," he barked, "I will take the shoulder straps off of every officer belonging to the regiment and dismount the regiment in disgrace."[29]

In addition to the military news in the fall of 1864, the nation's attention fell on the presidential election campaign, in which President Lincoln faced Democrat and former Union army general in chief George B. McClellan. Despite early doubts over his reelection, on November 8 Lincoln easily won a second term, defeating McClellan 212 to 21 in the Electoral College and garnering 55 percent of the popular vote. Lincoln's reelection was aided by the ballots of Union soldiers, who solidly supported the administration. A number of Northern states enacted provisions to allow soldiers to vote in the field, while many soldiers from states that had not enacted such laws were given leave in order to return home in time to cast their ballots. Though Black's surviving letters make no mention of the political campaign, his repeated comments of his desire to see the war through to its conclusion and the fact that his obituary described him as an ardent Republican and stated that at the time of his death he had voted for every Republican candidate for president after Millard Fillmore leave little doubt as to which candidate he supported. The men of the Twelfth Pennsylvania Cavalry voted decisively for the incumbent. According to one source, the regimental vote total was 321 for Lincoln and 184 for McClellan. One trooper in the Twelfth reported that in his company, thirty men voted for Lincoln and eleven for the "copperhead" or "rebel" ticket.[30]

* * *

Hd Quarters Co "G"
12. Pa. V. Cav
Bolivar Heights, Va,
Oct 21, 1864[31]
My Dear & much Loved Wife Jennie:
Again has it been my delight to receive from you another of those truly loving and cheering letters of yours. It is a source of great pleasure to me to hear from you so frequent[ly] and at every time as at this to have the gratifying news made known of your continued good health. It befalls my duty as well as pleasure to spend a few moments this very pleasant Autumn evening in responding and in doing so I will use my best efforts to give you the news in detail. It is mine to send forth the cheering news this evening to you, that Providence still favors me with continued good health, the best earthly gift a soldier can possess.

In my letter of the 19th Inst., I made mention of heavy cannonading being heard all day in the direction of Winchester, but then had not heard any news from there, beyond the reports of guns. Since then we have received word from it. Early in the morning Sheridan's Army was boldly attacked. The enemy took 16 pieces of artillery, and some prisoners. At 1 O'clock in the afternoon the tune changed, and our troops drove the enemy handsomely, capturing from them 43 pieces of Artillery, 2000 prisoners and quite a number of wagons, and entirely demoralized the rebel army. Sheridan claims it as one of the most glorious victories he ever achieved.[32] Sheridan is the man for the Shenandoah Valley.

I am pleased to hear that you attend Prayer Meeting. If I were at home I would go with you every night of meetings, I always did love to attend Prayer meetings.

Queer indeed that Skyles and Lue are such good friends again. I think they had better bring the matter to a final conclusion, get married and quit that courting. For my part I will leave them do as they like and then they will have no one to blame but themselves.

We are receiving new recruits for our regiment every day, to fill the place of those killed during the Summer Campaign. Our Company is as full as the law allows (103 men).

Well Jennie Dear as news is scarce I will draw to a close. Remember me kindly to Lue, mother, & Aunt, and my ever true undivided & devoted Love to you. While here I place my name as

> Your ever true devoted &
> affectionate Husband
> Lieut. John H. Black
> Co "G" 12. P.V. Cav
> Harpers Ferry, Va.

* * *

Camp 12. Pa. V. Cavalry
Camp Bolivar Heights, Va.
Oct. 27, 1864
My Dear & Much Loved Wife Jennie:

Good evening to you. It is quite a rainy evening, and cool too, but we need not complain, the time of year has come for such weather. . . .

Oh! Dear Jennie!!! You can hardly conceive how rejoiced I was this day on opening your letter to find your Photograph contained therein. It is far superior to the other, I think it almost natural. On looking at it, I think I can almost see my Dear standing before me. I prize it very highly and shall take the utmost care of it, and not have it lost as I had that likeness. But that was not my fault. . . .

I think [Lue] & Skyles had better make up their minds and have the "knot" tied, and not waste time so foolishly in sitting up at night, where they might be in the bed together, that is providing he would not go a soldiering. . . .

There is nothing new in the Valley, all is quiet for the present. We are getting along fine. On next Monday we will have a muster day again, after that the Paymaster but how soon we do not know.

So you are longing for winter to see *me* come home. Rest easy Jennie, the time will pass by, and that time will arrive and Oh! how pleased I will be, to be permitted to go home for a few weeks at least. It seems quite a while since I last saw you. It is drawing nigh unto 7 months. Still I presume according to your picture you look about as natural as ever. I can notice no changes in the least. . . .

> Your ever true, devoted &
> affectionate
> Husband
> Lieut. John H. Black
> Co. "G" 12. Pa. V. Cavalry
> Harpers Ferry, Virginia

* * *

Camp 12 Pa. V. Cavalry
Bolivar Heights, Va.
Oct. 30/64
My Dear & Loving Wife:

Good evening to you Jennie! As I have gone through with the regular routine of duty for the day, and night has come on, I find myself unemployed for the present, or in other words nothing special to do, in order that I may not be idle, I will devote those few moments in penning you a few lines. . . .

Sitting alone in my tent, meditating over the past, makes me heartily wish that I was with you this night, instead of being here, and I will know that you have the same wish this evening, particularly being it is Sunday evening, our favorite evening. I would rather be at home with you than here, although I cannot say anything against the service, for I glory in being a soldier. I am in great hope that this war will not continue long any more, and that I will be spared to return home to you. Oh! what a joyful meeting that would be, me returning home to stay. It is you that would almost be overjoyed and I could not be better pleased.

The weather is very pleasant, and I am in excellent health, with one slight exception. I have the toothache this evening. I presume it will be well by morning, at least I trust so. We are getting along very well, and are all in fine spirits.

Nothing new in the Valley. Rebels have grown scarce of late. We have not yet conceived any idea of going into winter quarters, and rather think we will not this winter. Time alone will disclose all those things. Tomorrow will be our muster day for pay, and after that the Paymaster, But no telling when thereafter. . . .

To you my ever true, devoted & undivided Love My Dear Wife Jennie, while at the same time I hereunto place my name

> as Your
> ever true, devoted &
> Affectionate
> Husband,
> Lieut. John H. Black
> Co. "G" 12. Pa. V. Cavalry
> Harpers Ferry, Virginia

* * *

The question of the reliability of the Pennsylvanians became so acute that by mid-December 1864 General Stevenson had requested the Twelfth be withdrawn from his forces and sent to the Army of the Potomac. Believing that this move "would be manifestly for the good of the service," Stevenson felt he could "get along with a smaller regiment in good discipline and with good officers."[33]

The appointment of regular army officer Marcus A. Reno to the colonelcy of the Twelfth Cavalry seemed to improve the unit's performance, or at least its discipline. In early February 1865, a party under Lt. Harlow Guild failed to capture a group of Rebels who had ambushed a Baltimore and Ohio train and then robbed its engineer. Guild bungled the pursuit, not following the route prescribed by his commander. As a result his force was fired upon by another group of the Twelfth Cavalry, and one trooper was wounded. An infuriated Reno arrested Guild and called for his immediate dismissal. He did not wish to court-martial the officer, reporting that a trial "would occupy more time than he is worth. He is entirely unfit for a commission, in as much as he takes no pains to improve himself, nor does he study to render himself worthy of his position. He, although never what you could charge as drunkenness, is always full, and when not stupefied with whiskey he is with opium. His performance last night is sufficient evidence against him to hang him."[34]

Despite the alleged incompetence of at least a portion of the Twelfth Cavalry, the regiment served in the Shenandoah Valley until the end of the war. The majority of officers and men in the unit, including John Black, served honorably in a very difficult situation. The increasing frustration of the Federals and growing desperation of the Confederates contributed to a brutalization of the fighting in the Shenandoah, which reached its peak in the second half of 1864 and early 1865. Atrocities, including the execution of prisoners, became more common. The period of the gentlemen's war had passed.

* * *

Camp 12. Pa. V. Cavalry
Charlestown, Va.
Dec. 5/64
My Dear Wife:
. . . Duty is none too severe. The weather is quite cool, just the kind of weather I enjoy best. Nothing new in the Valley, Rebels are scarce. I have not heard of any of late, except night before last, whilst I was on picket ten or so made their appearance. We fired a few shots at them and they left quicker than they came. No one hurt, it being too dark to take aim on the rascals. In my opinion everything is moving along very promising and I really believe that the rebellion is fast drawing to a close. I hope my opinion may be correct, for I long to see the end of this cruel war, that I may return home safe to my Jennie, never again to leave her while life remains.

No paymaster on hand, we are expecting every day. I heard this morning that he would be here this week for sure. Good for him I say. . . .

Your ever true, devoted &
Affectionate
Husband
Lieut. John H. Black
Co "G" 12 Pa. V. Cav.

* * *

Camp 12. Pa. V. Cavalry
Charlestown, Va.
Dec. 6, 1864
My Dear Wife:

Good evening to you. How are you this evening? I presume you are well, and sitting in the arm chair, all alone thinking about me and wondering how long it will be until I come home. I wish I could answer the question satisfactorily. I know it would be welcome to you, but that is beyond my power at present, so I will drop that question. . . .

The weather is very pleasant. We have what might be termed "*Indian Summer.*" It is us who can enjoy it in reality. Our duty is not very hard. We are getting along very well, have no reason whatever to complain. Everything quiet in the Valley, Rebels are not troubling us any. We are busy building stables for our horses. We have comfortable quarters for ourselves and will also have for the horses. If we should be so lucky as to remain here during the winter, we will undoubtedly have a pleasant time of it. But there is no knowing what may turn up, when we least expect it. . . .

> You ever true devoted &
> Affectionate
> Husband
> Lieut. John H. Black
> Co. "G" 12 Pa V. Cav

* * *

Camp 12. Pa. V. Cavalry
Charlestown, Va.
Dec. 8, 1864
My Dear Wife:

Quite a blustery evening, this, the weather has made a great change. Yesterday was perfect "Indian Summer." Today is real winter, the wind high, air very cold and the best place I can find is by the side of my stove. That is, when I am not on duty. But just as I finished the above line, the Adjutant came to my tent & told me that it falls my duty for Picket tomorrow morning, good for me for 24 hours. It is no hard duty, and only comes about once a week these times.

No sooner had the Adjutant gone than in steps the welcome mail carrier, a letter for me, eh! . . . First thing I notice in your letter is, that some of the boys are writing home that they intend reenlisting for five years, and also that John Walters[35] says he intends to do so. All right if they do so, then you tell me not to get that foolish notion in my head. No fears Jennie, and if ever I should, why you would be asked about it, and you saying no to it would settle the question for good. Had you not said yes, last winter when I asked the privilege to reenlist, I never should have reenlisted, but would be mustered out of service on the 18th of next February, with Sam O. Evans & a few others. Then, remember Dear, I was only your *lover,* but now, it is far different. Now I have more reason to listen to your advice than then, and as you well know I did then as you said I might. Remember Dear what that little word "yes" did then. I know that if asked again on the same question you will undoubtedly stick to the word of two syllables, which is plain "No" think you so?

Well! Well! Another visitor at my door. He brought to me this week's copy of our regimental paper. So with this letter I will send it, trusting that you had received the other copy ere this. I wonder whether I will have any more visitors as I close this epistle. Let them come. I will receive them courteously. . . .

Sam O. Evans is well. He is not with us at present. He is connected with the "Engineer Corps"[36] at Harpers Ferry, having a gay & joyful time. He will remain there until he is discharged. Barney is well. Everything is quiet in the Valley. Have not heard anything of rebels about for over a week past, except on the night of the 3rd while I was on duty of which I told you in a former letter. Jennie, no Paymaster yet with us, and no signs now for a month to come. I fear you are in need of money, if so, let me know in answer to this. I have near three hundred dollars at Fathers, and in case you need any I will write to him, to give it to you. Do not fear to tell me if you need it, for I am determined you & mother shall never want while I live. So be candid on answering, if you need it let me know. For my part I have enough with me to do me for several months yet & longer too. . . .

My ever true, devoted & undivided Love to you, while to this my name in real true sincerity as ever your, devoted &

Affectionate
Husband
Lieut. John H. Black
Co. "G" 12. Pa. V. Cav.

* * *

Camp 12 Pa. V. Cavalry
Charlestown, Va.
Dec. 20/64
My Dear & Loving Wife:

Alone in my humble soldier home this evening, I find that I can employ my leizure hours no more agreeably that inditing [?] a few lines to you. . . .

On Sunday morning at 6 o'clock we set out on a march and by evening we found ourselves in Winchester. Today we returned and this evening [is] my first opportunity to answer and so I will improve it indeed.

I was very happy indeed to learn of your good health, and can report myself to you the same, trusting that we may always have such good fortune. You appear to have plenty of snow & cold weather as well as we, and say Oh! how you would like to have me with you these cold nights. Remember there is another [who] wishes the same, but such cannot be the case at present & God only knows when it will be. About me getting home, I cannot tell you any more about it than before, no knowing when Furloughs will be granted. Not while the armies keep moving like they are at present. So Jennie rest easy and bear in mind that I will be at home to see you whenever I can get away. If it should so happen that I could not get home this winter the fault will be not mine, and therefore I will not be to blame. I would like very much to see you, but if not permitted to go, why it can't be helped.

Jennie rest as easy as you can. Take the world just as it comes, believing that all things work & move for good. About you coming to see me, that would be out of the question entirely. You might start and ere you reached this place we might be ordered away and not know where we would stop. All I care about is just so you take good care of yourself and are in good health. I will take all the care I can of myself, and ever keep you in my mind wherever I be.

That report about James Irvine, is so far as I know false. I am glad to hear that you are not in need of money, But do not fear to tell me when you are, for as I told you before you & mother shall never be in want, so long as it is my power to hinder it. It is for you that I live and wish to live.

Enclosed I send you another paper [the *Guidon*].[37] If you read the last week's [Hollidaysburg] Register you will see a notice of our papers. I sent one to the Editor.

Your ever true devoted &
affectionate
Husband
Lieut. John H. Black
Co. "G" 12. Pa. V. Cav.

P.S. Jennie Dear, Please send about a dozen or so of Stamps. There is no Post Office nearer than 8 miles and it is difficult for us to get any. I have a few yet, but they wont last long.

Your John

* * *

Camp, 12. Pa. V. Cavalry
Charlestown, Va.
Dec. 26, 1864
My Dear & Loving Wife:

Good morning to you. I trust you are well. Christmas is over and a gay and jolly time it was indeed to us. We had several roasted fowls and a variety of other good things, also a slight sprinkling of something good to drink in the shape of whiskey. It being the first I drank since the 21st of September last, I did not take an over dose, but had enough in me last night to make me feel a little "boozy." Excuse me Dear Jennie for doing so, I cannot help but tell you, I do nothing but what I will tell you of. . . .

I am pleased to hear that you are still in excellent health, trusting that such may continue to be your fortune. Did you have a Merry Christmas. I wish you a Happy New Year by day & pleasant dreams at night. So you did venture to have your fortune told, just as I would have done, would I have been there, and am pleased that she told you nothing bad. The children part is quite gay. I would not doubt but what that part might come true, as likely things as that have happened and may happen again. I know I will have no objections to it. I would liked to have been present when your fortune was being told. I could have amused myself and probably laughed somewhat, too. I see that you still express yourself much discontented, and feel lonely. I don't doubt your word in the least. I presume you will be so all the while I remain away from you.

You ask me one very nice little question, which is, whether I would not rather be at home with you than in the army. On the next page the answer. I would far rather be at home with you than here. Before we were married my inclinations for roving around were very great, but since then they have changed considerably and to tell you the candid truth that if we would have been married one year ago, I never could have had the idea of reenlisting at all. In that case I would be mustered out of service on the 17th of February next. But now it is different. When I reenlisted I told you in good faith that I would be promoted to a Lieutenancy and then in one year thereafter I would resign, but since my promotion General Grant issued an order refusing to accept resignations, except in case of disability. So you see where I am, and the fault is not mine. . . .

There was a sad affair took place yesterday in Company "E" of our Regiment. Two men of the company had some difficulty between themselves, and undertook to settle it by having a fight. The one proved treacherous and instead of resorting to blows with the fist, he drew his pistol and shot the other through the head, causing death in two hours. What a horrible thing it is to think of. The murderer is now in arrest and in all probability will meet his doom on the scaffold, which will be doing justice to him. I have no sympathy for him, and could not have for any murderer. . . .[38]

I am pleased to hear that Lue intends spending the Holidays in Duncansville. It will be quite a comfort to you in my absence. I trust you will enjoy yourselves together. Oh! But I wish I could be with you. It is three years since I have spent the last Christmas and New Year in your company, little thinking then that I would now be absent from you. I don't see how this war can continue one year longer. I wish it were over now. . . .

Some talk of us being paid this week, but only for the months of July & August. By the last of this month even if we do get two months pay we will have 4 months more due us. It will be good when it comes. One consolation we have if we don't it soon, we will not be liable to spend it very soon. If we get paid this week I will send you about one hundred dollars, but will write to you about it before I send it.

Everything is quiet in the Valley. No enemy to be seen or heard of. Duty is still very easy. No news of giving Furloughs yet. I wish they would soon commence granting them for I would very much like to pay you a visit about the latter part of next month, and have a gay & happy time with you a few days, I know we would enjoy ourselves. My word for it in truth, I will be at home the first opportunity I get, So if I cannot come, the fault will not be mine at all. Content yourself Dear Jennie as well as you can, be cheerful and look forward to the day when through the Will of God, I may return home safe to you. . . .

My name to this as
Your true, devoted, ever faithful
and Affectionate
Husband
Lieut. John H. Black
Co. "G" 12. Pa. V. Cav.

* * *

Camp 12. Pa. V. Cavalry
Charlestown, Va.
Dec. 28, 1864
My Dear Wife:

As the rain is rattling quite fast on the canvas roof of my humble tent I will employ a few spare moments in penning you some items although none of great importance, but by the by it may constitute a letter. This is not an answer to any one [of yours]. My health is exceedingly good and I am getting along so well that I have no reason to complain at all but on the other hand am thankful. The weather is rainy and the mud deep and plenty.

Jennie Dear I had a dream last night that I rather think I must relate to you as you were one of the characters in it. It was a very odd and also laughable one. I dreamed that I had obtained three days leave of absence and started home to see you. The first place I thought I landed was at Vaughns Old Tavern. There I got drunk and remained so for two days, & two nights. Then I took a notion I would take a walk down the road and see you. I did so, and found you scrubbing and spoke to you. I thought you turned around to me and told me coolly to go and spend that day & night where I had spent the last two. Without a word I turned around, went back to the Tavern, took a meal, and left for Camp by next train, and arrived safe in Camp, and then I wakened and found myself in Camp in bed. What possessed me to dream so I cannot tell, but so it was in my dream.

Everything is quiet in the Valley yet. Sergt. William J. Stiffler of our company, taken prisoner on the 1st of January 1864, died in Rebel Prison, Andersonville, Georgia on the 8th of May last. We were notified of it on the 26th Inst. by a 1st Sergt. of the 5th Iowa Cavalry, who was a fellow prisoner of Will's but is now exchanged and with his Regiment. Poor Stiffler, I could not help shedding tears when I heard it. He was a particular & warm friend of mine. I wrote a letter to his mother, and that an affectionate one too. I also wrote a piece for our Paper which you will see in the next one you receive.[39] Barney Engle, Sam O. Evans, Will Guin & Lundy are well and wish to be remembered to you. . . .

Your ever true devoted &
Affectionate
Husband
Lieut. John H. Black
Co. "G" 12. Pa. V. Cav.

* * *

Camp 12. Pa. V. Cavalry
Charlestown, Va.
Dec. 29, 1864
My Dear Wife:

Yesterday evening I wrote you a letter but did not get it mailed in consequence of the mail carrier leaving for the Ferry before his usual time. . . . I am well and have no reason to complain, except that I can not get that Furlough yet. I still live in hopes of getting it sometime. Better late than never. . . . I am pleased to hear that James Irvine has reached home. I am much obliged to you for those stamps. They come [in] very handy. The Paymaster is in Camp to night. He will commence paying tomorrow morning. It will take him about three days to pay us all.

So soon as paid I will express to you what I can spare. We only get two months pay this time. On Saturday we will be mustered for four months more.

My compliments to all inquiring friends. My love to you.

Your ever true devoted &
Affectionate Husband
Lieut. John H. Black
Co. "G" 12. P.V. Cav.

Chapter 5

1865

By early 1865 it appeared to most observers that the Confederacy was on the verge of collapse. Lincoln's reelection the previous November had dashed Southern hopes for a negotiated settlement to the war. Lee's Army of Northern Virginia, having withstood Grant's onslaught throughout the summer and fall, was stretched to the breaking point in its defensive lines around Petersburg. Gen. William T. Sherman, having presented Savannah to the nation as a Christmas present, prepared to embark on his destructive trek through the Carolinas. Defeatism, inflation, and shortages of food and supplies convinced many Southerners that the war was lost. Despite the grim outlook, Rebel forces continued to fight. In the Shenandoah Valley, John Mosby's partisans remained active, continuing their raiding and ambushing tactics, not withstanding their commander's severe wounding in December 1864.

The Twelfth Pennsylvania Cavalry, along with the other Union forces in the valley, continued their frustrating attempts to clear the area of Mosby's men. John H. Black passed a relatively quite winter, much of it spent at Harpers Ferry on court-martial duty. No doubt he hoped that 1864–65 would be the last winter he had to spend away from his beloved Jennie.[1]

* * *

Camp 12. Pa. Vol. Cavalry
Charlestown, Virginia
January 1, 1865
My Dear & Loving Wife:
. . . The New Years day is nearly gone by. It was quite a happy one to me, but far happier would it have been had I spent it in company with you my Dear Wife. Oh! but I do wish I was at home with you these days. What a happy time we could have, indeed. The weather is very cold, [with] snow on the ground again. It is the very thing for me. I would always rather have cold weather & snow in winter than warm, wet, & muddy.

Well Jennie Dear, the long looked for & anxiously expected Paymaster has at last visited us, & was kind enough to pay us two months wages, when there was actually six months due us. On yesterday we were mustered for the other four months, and no knowing when we will be paid, nevertheless I don't care a great deal with what I did receive I can send a portion to you. Don't know exactly how much, not less than $75 and will have a good share for myself. If I could have received the six month's pay at the one time I could have quite a sum for you. What I have to send to you this time, I will express tomorrow and enclose the receipt for the amount in this letter. You can receive it at the same place you received the last, and as soon as received let me know. I send it to you as a New Year's Gift, although it will be rather late. Don't forget mother when it reaches you. . . .

I have very easy times at present. On the 27th of last month I was detailed as a member of the Board of General Court Martial.[2] We are on duty five days each week, and but three hours each day, and have the rest of the time entirely to ourselves. Our meetings are held at Harpers Ferry. We expect it to continue for three months, it may be longer & it may not be so long. Our duty consists in trying all cases of enlisted men, for desertion, disobedience of orders, &c. That murder case I mentioned in a former letter will come before us in the course of a week or so. So you see I am free of scouts and picket duty at the present and will be so long as we remain in session. Ain't I a lucky fellow. . . .

> Your ever true, devoted &
> Affectionate
> Husband
> Lieut. John H. Black
> Co. "G" 12. Pa. V. Cavalry

* * *

Camp 12. Pa. V. Cavalry,
Charlestown, Va.
Jan. 5/65
My Dear Wife:

It is mine on this a very cold & bleak winter evening, while alone in my tent to acknowledge the receipt of another of your favors. . . .

I am perfectly aware that you are laboring under great discontentment in regard to me. . . . I would if it were in my power (for your sake alone) leave the service immediately, but dear Jennie it is altogether beyond my control and power. Many is the night after I lay me down in my humble soldier cot, that I get to studying about you, and me being absent from you. While so studying often do the tears come unbidden. I like the service, and were it not for you my dearest earthly friend I would always be a soldier, but no, I will not always be a soldier. At my first honorable opportunity I will quit the service and return to you, but bear in mind never dishonorably, for the latter would break my heart. Oh! had I not reenlisted on the 17th of next month I could and would claim my discharge and return to you but it is too late and that is over. So we will let that pass by and hope for the best the Lord being our guide.

I am sorry to learn that you did not have a merry Christmas. If I would have been there you would have had, for I know I could have made it a happy one for you.

So you say that James Irvin is cutting quite a dash among the ladies. Good for him. Did he ever tell you how he happened to get wounded? It was not in battle it was merely an accidental shot in camp made to by himself. At least his lieutenant told me so a few days ago. That is all I know about it. I am pleased to hear that Mr. Lovell has become a professor of religion. I trust that he will live a life in accordance with his profession and be a useful man in the community. I wish you & I were Christians.[3] Would it not be joyful? . . .

I sent you $100 on last Monday which I presume you have received. It is entirely at your disposal, just you get what you need and think proper for yourself and mother and bear in mind I will be satisfied. . . .

You see by the last paper I sent you that our Colonel left us. Since then we have had the honor to have a new one appointed. Reno, I believe is his name. He came to camp this evening. He is a young man, but a bright chap I presume.[4]

I am much obliged to you for those stamps. You need not send me any more as I am on duty at the Ferry and can get plenty at the office. I have gay & easy times.

That New Year's kiss is accepted with a thousand thanks, trusting that I can give you a real one in return ere many weeks. Would it not be pleasant? . . .

Lieut. John H. Black

* * *

Harpers Ferry, Va.
January 11, 1865
Dear Wife:

. . . I am getting along very well and have no reason to complain whatever, but on the other hand have reason to be very thankful that it is as well with me as it is. This has been a very pleasant day, yesterday it rained without ceasing. Tomorrow may be a cold & blustery day as far as I know. The weather changes with us in an hours time. No telling one day what will be the next. You will see by the heading of this letter that I am at the Ferry instead of Charlestown, and intend to remain here for some time to come. Excuse this short letter. Remember me to mother & aunt.

My love to you while to this my name

as your ever true devoted &
affectionate
Husband.
Let. John H. Black
Co. "G"

* * *

Camp 12. Pa. Vol. Cavalry
Charlestown, Va.
January 12, 1865
My Dear Wife:

This evening I left the Ferry on a visit to Camp. Tomorrow morning I will go back to the Ferry again. . . .

I am happy to learn that the money reached you in safety. Your thanks for the same are kindly accepted, knowing that they were kindly given.

I am sorry to learn that poor Moses Garland[5] had been numbered among the dead. He had followed his wife to her long home. . . .

So Jim Irvin is sick, queer indeed that so many who go home on leave, get sick about the time their leave expires and then get their leaves extended. It is getting quite fashionable among them be it. Queer indeed Barney did not send his mother some money. He received $82, and I really think he should have sent her a portion at least one half. He is quite a spendthrift and will spend it all in a few weeks time if he does not send it home.

The weather was quite pleasant today. I enjoy it very much. I am getting along admirably well, very easy duty indeed. You still express yourself very much discontented. I am well aware of it, and believe every word you say. Oh! But I would love to gratify your wish in regard to seeing me come home on a visit. I make you this promise now that I made you before that at my first opportunity I will come home, and I trust it will soon be. I am still confident that I will get home yet ere Spring. I may be mistaken but I really think that I am not. Content yourself as well as you can and hope for the bet & so will I.

Everything is quiet in the Valley. No move of any kind going on at present. The troops are all enjoying themselves, not much duty for anyone. Evans, Barney, Gwin and Lundy are well. Evans will be mustered out of service the 17th of next month and will then return to civil life, I wish I could go with him. Oh! would not that be joyful news then to you & me. But here I am a veteran. . . .

My ever true devoted & undivided Love to you, while my name to this as, your ever true devoted & affectionate

Husband
Lieut. John H. Black
Co "G" 12 Pa. V. Cav.

P.S. I will write again on Saturday and send another paper.

* * *

Harpers Ferry, Va.
January 13, 1865
My Dear Wife:
This is not intended as a letter, just simply a note accompanying a copy of our paper.
You will notice that our new Colonel received quite a flattering notice in its columns. No doubt he is richly deserving it. In my humble opinion he is an excellent officer, and a gentleman.
Weather is pleasant. Everything quiet. My Love to you.
Your true, devoted &
Affectionate
Husband
Lieut. John H. Black
Co. "G" 12. Pa. Cavalry

* * *

Harpers Ferry, Va.
January 17, 1865
My Dear Wife:
I am still at the Ferry on duty for 3 hours each day and I am well pleased with my position, couldn't be better pleased while in the service. The only objection I have to my duty here is that while this court lasts I cannot get home but so soon as it adjourns I think I will be all right. I am real confident that I will get off between this and Spring. An order has reached our Regiment granting Furloughs of 15 days, So that when you see me coming home you may expect me to stay for that time. Rest easy and content yourself. All will be right. The prospects are bright before us. I begin to think the war is fast drawing to a close and peace is not so far off as some might think. I have no idea of spending another year in this service.
Everything is quiet in the Valley, as quiet as ever. Our new Colonel is drilling the Regiment and getting along with it splendidly. We are expecting the Paymaster here next week to pay us the 4 months due us. I will be pleased to see him.
Remember me kindly to Lue, and tell her I heard she was going to get married, and tell her I wish she may & get a kind husband and never have a quarrel with [him] while she
lives. . . .

Take good care of yourself. . . . Be gay & cheerful, let time glide by swiftly, and some of these days when you are not looking for me you will see me coming home. . . .

My ever true devoted & undivided Love to you.

While my name to this as

> Your ever true devoted &
> Affectionate
> Husband Lieut. John H. Black
> Co. "G" 12 Pa. V. Cav.

* * *

Camp 12. Pa. Cavalry
January 20, 1865
My Dear Wife Jennie:

Good evening to you, with a polite bow, trusting you are well. You will see by the above that I am in Camp again. I came out on the train this evening on a visit and will return to the Ferry in the morning. I found the boys all getting along very well. I did not see James Irvine yet, but I heard that he has returned. I may see him in the morning. . . .

Jennie, I cannot tell you yet when I will be at home, but as I told you before I am confident that I will get home ere the Spring Campaign opens. I am still on duty at the Ferry and may be for several months yet. It is quite easy duty and no risks to run. I have quite easy times. . . .

I saw Sam O. Evans yesterday evening. He is well & wishes to be remembered to you. Barney Engle is well & getting along finely, but I understand he did not send any money to his mother the last pay day. I asked him his reason. He gave me no reply, and so I left him alone, probably he knows best.

Evans is making an effort to be mustered out of service next week. I trust he will be successful. The weather is quite cold yet. We have become accustomed to it and do not mind it in the least. I will send you this weeks "Guidon" by Monday's mail. It will not be printed in time to send by this letter.

Oh! But I would like to be at home with you tonight. It would be far better than going to bed alone on a cold and stormy night. I presume you think the same too. But so it is and it must be borne. . . .

> Your true, devoted & affectionate
> Husband
> Lieut. John H. Black
> Co. "G" 12. Pa. Cavalry

* * *

Harpers Ferry, Va.
Jan. 22, 1865
My Dear Wife:

Good morning to you. How are you this Sunday morning? I presume you are about going to Sabbath School. I wish I were to accompany you. It has been a long time since I last attended any such a place. In April last I believe. In this land of tumult, uproar and contention, Sunday School would be a novelty. . . .

I will endeavor to . . . give you what little news there is afloat, which in fact is unusually scarce, more so than any time while I am [in] Virginia. . . .

[I] will have this for Monday's mail, and, with it, send you the 8th number of the "Guidon." The weather is quite rough today, raining and sleeting in full earnest. Everything is quiet in the Valley. The troops are enjoying their winter quarters. Barney Engle is well. I saw him yesterday. A rumor afloat this morning that the Paymaster will be about this week. He will be welcomely received and treated with respect. . . .

Last but not least, my true, devoted & undivided Love to you my Dear Wife, while to this I annex my name as your ever true devoted and

> Affectionate
> Husband
> Lieut. John H. Black
> Co. "G" 12. Pa. Cavalry
> *Harpers Ferry, Va.*

* * *

Camp 12th Pa. Cavalry
Charlestown, Va.
January 28/65
Dear Wife:

Good evening to you. Quite a cold evening too. You will see by the above that I am on a visit to Camp again. I will go back to the Ferry on tomorrow noon train. . . .

So you are looking for me home, and here I am not knowing when I will get off. One thing certain I will not get away before the General Court martial closes. How long it will continue I cannot tell. It may close in a week and may not close for two months. . . .

The weather is most intensely cold, and no cessation thereof apparently. I never knew of such concentration of cold weather. . . . Sergt. David M. Ginter [sp?][6] of our Company left for home on Furlough of 15 days on day before yesterday. He said he would call and see you before he returned.

Did you hear anything of Jacob Walters, whether he was exchanged with that John Brissell[7] of our Company. I would like to see Jacob return to the Company. He could be mustered out on the 17th of next month if he were here. Barney Engle is well & getting along finely. He told me this evening that he sent his Mother $40. last pay day. Do you know whether she received it or not? Will Gwin is well & also Sam O. Evans. Will Gwin will be mustered out with Evans.

Everything is quiet in the Valley. Every body is getting the opinion that the war will not last many months more. I trust that it is true what they think.

> Your ever true, devoted &
> affectionate
> Husband
> Lieut. John H. Black
> Co "G"

* * *

Camp 12. Pa. Cavalry
Charlestown, Va.
February 10/65
My Dear Wife:
    . . . I have better hopes now of getting home than I have had this winter for the simple reason that the General Court Martial of which I was a member is dissolved and I have returned to my Regiment, and am now assured by the Colonel that I will get a furlough in the course of 4 or 5 *weeks*. So all right. So be in good cheer Dear Jennie, if my life and health are so long spared you may positively expect to see me at home on leave of 15 days some time in the month of March. Oh! but I long for the time to come, for I am getting pretty much as you say you are. I am getting anxious to see you & cannot rest until I do see you and spend a

few and very pleasant & happy days with you. You need not look for me on the arrival of the trains until I send you word that I will be at home in the course of a short time from the date of such notice. . . .

Quite a sad affair will take place at Harpers Ferry, Va on Friday the 17th Inst. Five men (soldiers) are to [be] shot to death for Desertion.[8] They were tried and sentenced by our court. They belong to New York Regiments. It is hard but I must say it is nothing more than justice. . . .

A portion of our Company were on a scout a few days ago, and had a slight Skirmish, in which one man of Co "G" by the name of John Frye[9] was killed. The boys killed one Reb and wounded two and came off victorious. We buried the man of our Company by the honors of war today. . . .

> Your ever true, devoted &
> affectionate
> Husband
> 1st Lieut. John H. Black
> Co. "G" 12. Pa. Cav.

* * *

Camp 12. Pa. Cav.
Charlestown, Va.
Feb. 14, 1865
Dear Wife:

. . . The weather is still on the cold order. In my opinion we have [had] a full share of winter this year. All the better, for the colder the winter is the healthier it is. . . .

I was very much disappointed to hear that Dave Gildae [?][10] had given up the idea of going into the army. It is queer indeed that Dave is satisfied with but 3 months duty as a soldier for his country's cause. It appears to me that I could not forgive myself if I had served but three months. For my part, I have done more & for your sake if I could get out of service honorably I would quit right off, but if I ever live to get out of service alive it will be honorably. I have resolved to obey all orders and do my duty as a soldier and I find I get along a great deal better than those who are always finding fault.

Your congratulations in regard to my promotion are kindly accepted. In a few days I will send you my commission and other papers thereunto belonging for safe keeping, for I know you are the one to take good care of anything for me.[11] I saw Henry Will [?][12] this evening, he called on me. He is getting along very well. He is well liked by all who know him. His Capt. promoted him to Sergt. Today. He will make an excellent one too.

You asked me who has my place in the Company. By examining the paper of last week that I send enclosed, you will see that the name is spelled McGuff in the paper, but the proper way to spell it is McGough.[13] He will make an excellent officer.

About getting home, you may depend upon me getting home in March some time. The Capt. goes home in a few days. When he returns I will get off. So rest easy, you will get to see me in not very long. So be in good health Jennie. I will be about.

Evans will be mustered out Friday of this week also Will Gwin. Barney Engle is well, Lundy is well.

Your ever true devoted
& affectionate
Husband
1st Lieut. John. H. Black
Co. "G" 12. P Cav

* * *

Camp 12. Pa. Cav.
Charlestown, Va.
February 20/65
Dear Wife:
. . . This is quite a pleasant day. The snow is fast disappearing. It cannot stand the Sun. I am well and getting along very smoothly. Have quite easy times, But have not yet succeeded in getting that Furlough. I don't know how soon I may get it. Capt. McAteer leaves for home tomorrow on fifteen days leave. It appears that my time has not come yet. I presume that it will be forthcoming. Everything is quiet at present. We do something at drilling when the weather permits.

On Friday last I went to the Ferry to witness the execution of two soldiers, tried and sentenced to be shot to death for Desertion. They were brought out according to order, under the tune of the death march, and after the ministers prayed with them for a half hour they kneeled by the black coffins and prayed themselves, then arose and bid each other goodbye. After that their hands were tied behind their backs, [and] the sentence of death read to them.

They then took their seats on the foot of the coffins, each facing ten men who were armed [and] ready to receive the word to fire. At this critical moment in came a fleet horseman bearing a dispatch. On opening and reading it proved to be a reprieve. The Genl. then rode forward & informed the boys that they were pardoned. You had better think they were pleased. They walked towards each other and shook hands again with joy. They were not the only ones that rejoiced, everyone present was pleased. They marched from there with lighter hearts than they came with. I don't think they will ever desert again while they live. There were about 3000 present, soldiers and citizens.[14]

Nothing more But my choicest love to you. My name to this as your ever true devoted &

> affectionate
> Husband
> 1st Lieut. John H. Black
> Co "G"

P.S. Enclosed you will find my commission and a few other Documents which you will please take care of. JHB

* * *

Camp 12. Pa. Cavalry
Charlestown, Va.
February 21/65
My Dear & Loving Wife:

I see by your letter that you are still discontented and very anxious to see me come home. Well Jennie Dear, in truth to you, I have made every effort thus far to get away, and have not yet succeeded, and no knowing when I may. I trust they will not postpone it too long. It will not be over one month before the Spring campaign will open in this section and then chances to get home will cease.

Still I am in hopes that I will get away yet. If I do not Dear Jennie, (whatever you do), do not blame me, for really it will not be my fault. I am very anxious to see you, and be with you a few days. You complain of the nights being so cold. I would like to be with you at present. It would not be so cold then. Don't you think I am right?

... Mrs. Engle need not look for Barney at present. I do not think he will get home this winter. I do not think he wants to go home. You need not tell her so. . . . Enclosed I will send you the paper last week. You will notice the muster out of some of Co. G. Everything is quiet in this section of the army.

Oh! Jennie, I am in good hopes of the war closing this Summer coming. Our army is successful everywhere. Oh! then I can return to you for good. What joyful times those will be. . . .

> My ever true undivided &
> devoted
> Love to you. . . .
> 1st Lieut. John H. Black
> Co. "G"

* * *

Camp 12. Pa. Cavalry
Feb. 23, 1865
Dear Wife:

Good afternoon to you. With us the weather is very muddy. The snow is thawing and it is also raining. No doubt you are aware how our Camp looks amid all that. One consolation we have on a rainy day, and it is only one that is there is no drilling to be done. For my part I would rather see fair weather than the way it is.

. . . I can report myself as heretofore in excellent health and getting along very well in every way, but getting a leave of absence to go home. I have not got that yet and no knowing when I will get it. It really appears to me that I am not to get home this Spring, and I cannot tell the reason why. I have [made] effort time & again and all is of no avail so far. I will not give it up yet, but will persevere until the last. I may be fortunate enough yet.

. . . News from our Southern armies is excellent. If Sherman continues on a while as he has done for the last few months, I don't think there will be much fighting to be done. The Soldiers all are thinking about getting home for good sometime next Summer. Would that not be glorious. I trust is may be so.

> Your ever true devoted and
> Affectionate
> Husband
> 1st Lieut. John H. Black
> Co. "G" 12. Pa. Cav.

* * *

Camp 12. Pa. Cavalry
Charlestown, Va.
March 2, 1865
Dear Wife:

. . . I can report myself in as good health as ever and getting along very well in every way except in the way of getting a "leave of absence" to go home. In that latter I have so far failed, nevertheless I have not given it up yet, but will try until the last, and if I fail Dear Jennie do not blame me at all, for my word for it I am very anxious to see you. Great report that you give about the soldier's wifes at home. I presume they get cold these cold nights and think a bedfellow a good thing to keep them warm, that is providing they lay right close together, as such bedfellows generally do, when sleeping in a bed. . . .

That is quite a queer way of courting poor Charley Gardner[15] had to follow while at home. I would not fancy such a way. Indeed I would not undertake to keep company with a girl that I could not go to her home to see her.

Everything is quiet at present. Rainy weather and mud plenty. . . .

> Your ever true devoted &
> Affectionate
> Husband
> 1st Lieut. John H. Black
> Co. "G"

* * *

Camp 12. Pa. Cavalry
Charlestown, Va.
March 6, 1865
My Dear Wife:

You mentioned about receiving a paper [the *Guidon*]. I presume it will be the last one you will get of that kind. The establishment is closed, the men who were carrying it on, were wanted for duty and consequently had to quit work, and so it closed up.

Now about the getting home. It is with sorrow that I have to acquaint you of the fact that it is all over for this time. On Saturday last an order reached the Regiment saying there would be no more Furloughs granted, and as I had not yet had mine granted, it came under that order, and here

I am only to tell you that you need not look for me home this Spring, because it is now out of the question.[16] I well know that this news will grieve you and no doubt cause you to take a *cry,* but indeed I can't and could not help it. I have never been so sadly disappointed since I have been in the Army, so Dear Jennie content yourself as well as you can and live in hopes of the war ending during the coming Summer, & in the hope of me getting home safe to you ere another winter and that to remain with you. . . . You can tell Mrs. Engle that She need not look for Barney home this Spring. He is now in the same fix I am. He cannot get away since the order is issued.

The news of the Valley is very encouraging this evening. The rumor is that General Sheridan attacked the rebel General Early at Charlotteville [*sic*], Va. and captured him & his Staff officers and 1800 men. Good for the gallant Sheridan. It appears that our troops are victorious wherever they go nowadays.[17]

So Jennie I tell you again be of good cheer. This war will close ere long and you & I may by the kindest of Providence, be permitted to spend many happy days together yet. . . .

> Your ever true devoted &
> Affectionate
> Husband
> Lieut. John H. Black
> Co "G' 12. Pa. Cavalry

* * *

Camp 12. Pa. Cavalry
Charlestown, Va.
March 12/65
My Dear Wife:

. . . It is not in my power to give you a letter of much length this time as news is very scarce, but such as is afloat I will give you. You state that you have not seen anything of Sam O. Evans. I have learned that he is 2nd Lieut., in the 16th Pa. Cavalry. I am pleased to hear that Will Gwin called to see you. James P. Stewart[18] has returned to the Company, and did not find time to call on you. The going home question as I told you before is "played out" for this time. . . .

Do not trouble yourself much about coming Summer. I do not think it is a going to be a rough campaign. I am getting in better hopes every day about the war soon closing. It cannot close too soon for me. You are well aware of that.

The weather is very favorable. The mud is fast drying away. We had quite a grand Regimental Drill today, we made quite a display. The boys are all mounted on good horses & well prepared for the field, and may be called on any day to forward march.

We are not troubled by rebels in this section at present. . . .

> My ever true devoted &
> undivided
> Love to you. . . .
> 1st Lieut. John H. Black
> Co "G"

* * *

Camp 12. Pa. Cav.
Charlestown, Va.
March 15, 1865
My Dear Wife:

. . . I am getting along very well have no reason to complain of anything but that I did not get my leave. . . . I live in hopes that the war is fast drawing to a close and then I trust that I will be among the number to return home safe and sound. . . .

I am sorry to hear that [the] Walters have not heard anything from Jacob. I fear he has met his fate of many others that were confined in rebeldom. Poor fellow if it is so. I trust & hope that he will yet be heard from, when the rest of the prisoners arrive.

Another man of Company "G" was sent to his long home. On last week a few of our scouts were out on a tour and came across a few rebels, had a brisk fight, resulted in killing one man (James E. McHugh)[19] [of] Co. "G" and wounding one of Co. "M" and capturing two others.[20] Our boys wounded six of them. News from all the Departments of our Army is very encouraging. It causes the soldiers to be jubilant and gleeful. . . .

> Your ever true devoted &
> Affectionate
> Husband
> John H. Black
> 1st Lieut. Co. "G" 12. Pa. Cav.

* * *

The approach of spring brought an increase in military activity in the lower Shenandoah Valley. On March 17, Col. Marcus Reno of the Twelfth Cavalry received instructions from Maj. Gen. Winfield S. Hancock, commanding the Middle Military Division at Winchester, to mount an expedition into Loudoun County in search of Confederate guerrillas.[21]

On the morning of March 20, Reno led a force of about one thousand men out from Harpers Ferry. His command consisted of the First United States Veteran Infantry, the Twelfth Cavalry, and the Loudoun County Rangers. This latter organization was composed of loyal Virginians who had formed themselves into a Union cavalry unit. The Rangers had proven to be quite effective in counter-guerrilla operations against Mosby and other Confederate bands.

After encamping at Hillsboro on the night of March 20–21, the column moved on to Purcellville, with the cavalry passing through Leesburg, Waterford, and Wheatland. On both days the Federals skirmished with Mosby's Rebels, while also "destroying what forage could be found in the possession of disloyal persons."[22]

With his command concentrated at Purcellville, Reno pushed on toward Hamilton, also known as Harmony, a small hamlet west of Leesburg. Confederate resistance increased as the Federals approached the village. Briscoe Goodheart of the Loudoun Rangers described the situation: "The column marched down the pike towards Hamilton, and the rebels marched along parallel with our column, but kept about a half a mile away. They were also in our advance and rear about the same distance. Whenever a hill or ravine would protect them they would crawl near enough to the road to bushwack us, and we kept out a skirmish line on each side and rear, and an advance guard to prevent a surprise."[23]

John Mosby had gathered about 120 of his command at Hamilton to contest the Yankee advance. Posting the bulk of his forces about one mile south of town on the road to Silcott Springs, he sent six riders toward Hamilton to try to draw the Federal cavalry into his trap. Taking the bait, the bluecoat horsemen impetuously charged down the pike after the Confederates. Lt. John H. Black led the chase. Regimental historian Larry Maier wrote that Black "commanded the Regiment's vanguard and . . . probably should have known better than to be lured into those forbidding woods by that well-worn ploy."[24]

Approaching a small rise, the Yankees were astonished when Mosby's main force attacked them from the front and flank. In a brief, swirling melee, the Federals lost nine killed and twelve wounded before retreating to the safety of their infantry, with the Rebels in hot pursuit. A volley from the foot soldiers drove the Confederates off. Sgt. John Casner of the Twelfth left a graphic account of the confused engagement:

> We followed them into a woods at the south of the town. I was with the advance when we were surprised by a large band of ambushing guerrillas, whom we had left camp to capture.
>
> In the confusion we were merged into a hand-to-hand fight. I was riding along when a rebel suddenly wheeled, aimed, and ordered me to surrender. I raised my revolver and fired instead. His horse reeled and threw him off. I passed Capt. [sic] Black, of Co. E [sic], lying wounded by the road-side. I saw a rebel Captain firing into our men and doing deadly work. I fired and wounded him. . . . [25]

During hand-to-hand combat with Charles Wiltshire of Mosby's command, Black was unhorsed and left on the ground "badly stunned" by a pistol ball that entered the small of his back above the right hip. The wound evidently affected Black's spine, paralyzing his legs. Black was left behind in Southern hands when the Union forces retreated. Although a Confederate participant later remembered Black as "the gallant lieutenant" who had led the charge, this did not stop the Rebels from strip-ping him of all his valuables and leaving him clad in only "pan-taloons, shirt, and drawers."[26]

No doubt because of the seriousness of his wound, Mosby's men did not keep Black prisoner. It is unclear how or by whom, but the wounded officer was placed in the home of a Unionist family in Loudoun County. They would care for him until he could be moved. A shocked Jennie Black received the news of her husband's wounding in a brief telegram.[27] Initial reports had been received in Pennsylvania that Black had been killed in the

Hamilton fight, and in fact several newspapers had carried announcements of his death.

Black would remain in the hands of two different pro-Union families until early May, when he was able to travel to Harpers Ferry for further convalescence. John Black never again served with the Twelfth Cavalry. As soon as it was safe to do so, Jennie traveled to Harpers Ferry to be with John. Her obituary later noted: "Mrs. Black was summoned to Harper's Ferry, where her husband, who had been severely wounded, was a patient at a private house. A couple of weeks afterward they returned [home to Pennsylvania] and have never been away from each other since."[28] While Black recuperated, the Twelfth moved to the vicinity of Winchester, Virginia. It stayed there until July 20, when, with the cessation of hostilities, the men were mustered out of the service. On the muster-out roll for Company G, Black was listed as "absent sick on account of a severe gun shot wound received in action at Hamiltonville, Loudoun County, Va. March 21, 1865."[29]

After having served on active duty for four years, Black fell wounded in his regiment's last significant combat action. While the other survivors of the Twelfth quickly began the transition from military to civilian life, John Black was left with the agony of his wound, and the realization that his life would never be the same as it had been before the war. Black would survive, but he was left a semi-invalid for the remainder of his life. While the skirmish at Hamilton did not rank with the great battles of the war, to John Black and a few of his comrades it was just as costly.

* * *

Charlestown, Virginia
March 31, 1865
Miss Jennie Black,

I received your Dispach [sic] this day and answered it immediately but could not explane [sic] to you in the Dispach all in regard to your Dear Husband. He was badly wounded on Tuesday 21, March in a fight at Hamilton, Loudoun Co., Va. I left him on Saturday last. He was getting along very well considering his wound. I think he will get well, I do hope he will. In him I have lost a good officer and a brave soldier. When he was wounded I had but little hope of his recovery but there are hopes now. I will let you know as soon as I hear from him. He is fifteen miles frome [sic] hear [sic]. He's with a good union family and will be well cared for, and as soon as he is able to be moved he will be brought to Harpers ferry. He told me when I left him to have his money sent home to you which was done as soon [as] I returned.

Yours very respectfully,
P. H. McAteer
Capt Co G
12. Pa Vol Cavalry

* * *

Ebensburg April 4th 1865
Dear Cousin:[30]

Your letter came to hand yesterday and the news that it brought is truly Sad. Dear Cousin [I] feel Sorry and my heart of hearts for you and the dear companion of you[r] heart but let us try and hope that it is not as bad as represented. My prayer to God is that he may recover if he is Still alive. Dear Jane I cannot tell you how I felt when I first heard that Black was killd [sic]. It went through me like a knife but this is the fate of war. If I knowed [sic] what to do for you that would lessen your trouble and grief I would freely do it but that vacant place is hard to fill but I hope and trust that he may be restored to you again and that you may live to see many happy days in each others society. You desire me to come down to See you as soon as possible well I can not Set any time at present but will come as Soon as I can. Pleas [write] and let us know every few days wether [sic] you hear any thing from John. Dear Jane let us all look to that God who is always redy [sic] to help in time of nead [sic] and trouble and let us unite in asking God for the recovery of you[r] dear husband. This is my Prayer in his behalf. Nothing more this time but wite Soon. This from your Symphathysing cousin

William & Mary Leighty[31]

* * *

Loudoun County, Virginia
April 8, 1865
My Dear Wife:

Undoubtedly you have heard through my friends in Camp of the misfortune that befell me on Tuesday the 21st of March. [I was so badly]

wounded that I had to be left behind when the Regiment returned to Charlestown.

It is now my good fortune to report to you that I am recovering rapidly and in a few day[s] expect to leave here on a trip to the Ferry. As soon as I reach the Ferry I will again write to you. I would have written to you before but had no opportunity of sending it. A friend of mine will see that this crosses the river between this & Monday. Do not get uneasy about me. My wound is not dangerous, any more. It was rather so at first. Jennie, do not trouble yourself about me not having good care taken of me. Although I was left here entirely among strangers they proved to be good Union friends. I received every care & attention that could be bestowed on any one.

I have been at two different houses. The first place I was at was an old lady & her three daughters. They treated me as a mother & sisters would treat a person. I remained there two weeks getting better, but not well enough to stand a trip over the River, and for fear some rebels might chance along and move me South, I was one night moved to where I now am. Here I am receiving every care & attention that can be given anyone. So do not on that score trouble yourself at all. Just be thankful, as I am that my life was spared at all. When I fell from my horse, wounded, I thought my day was sealed, but good care & attention saved me. I never shall forget those who took such great interest in my behalf.

Remember me to Mother & Aunt kindly & please let the folks at home know that you received this note from me. My wound gives me no pain at all, I rest quite easy. The wound was made by a pistol ball above the right hip in the small of the back. When the ball struck me, both my legs & and in fact all of the part of my body below the wound was paralyzed. That is what has disabled me so. I am speedily recovering from that and hope soon to be able to walk again.

> My love to you
> While my name to this as your
> true, devoted,
> & affectionate
> Husband
> John H. Black

P.S. I will write in a few days when I get over the river. JHB

* * *

There are included in the John H. Black Collection several letters written to Jennie by Black's comrades in the Twelfth, in addition to the letters written to John from his friends outlining the last several months of the regiment's service.

* * *

Camp 12 P.V.C.
Near Winchester Va
April 9/65
Mrs. Jennie Black:

Your letter dated April 1 was received a few days ago but being on the march then and ever since I was unable to answer sooner, but as this is the earliest opportunity I will improve it and answer your letter to the best of my knoweldge [sic]. The Captain also received a letter from you and would have answered but as I am writing [sic] he thought it unnecessary. As we have been on the march ever since I wrote you we have been unable to hear anything at all about your husband. You wished to know where he was wounded. The ball entered his body on the right side passing near the spine and comeing [sic] out on the left side. The Captain saw him the third day after he was wounded. He was much better then and in good hopes of getting well soon and the doctors all said he will get well soon.

You also wished to know where he is and if you can get to him. He is at a citizens house near Hamiltonville, Loudon County, and about 25 miles from Harpers Ferry, and I think you can get to him if you undertake to come to see him. You can come to Harpers Ferry by railroad and go to General Stevenson's[32] Head Quarters (He is the Commanding General there) and inquire for Captain Grubb.[33] He is Capt of the Loudon [R]angers. He is acquainted with the people where he is and he will assist you in getting to see your husband. It is impossible for me to get to Harpers Ferry or I would meet you at the Depot and go with you to General Stevensons Hd Qrs.

Capt Grubb says it is a good Union mans house that he is at and that he will be well taken care of. As it is getting late I will close. If there is any other information I can give you it will be a great pleasure to me so to do. There is four letters here for the Lieut. What shall I do with them. Please write soon and let me know if you have heard anything from Lieutenant and if I hear anything I will write.

I remain your Sincere well wisher.
James P. Stewart
Co "G" 12 Pa. Vol Cav
Winchester, Va

P.S. Please excuse this miserable letter as it is raining and the water is dropping through the tent as you can see from the appearance of this paper.

J. P Stewart

* * *

Loudoun County, Virginia
May 1, 1865
Dear Wife:

Again do I undertake to indite [?] you a few hasty lines. [I am] [s]till in the above named County about 18 miles from Harpers Ferry. I had thought when I wrote you last that by this time I would have been over the River, but am not yet. I suppose you think it very strange that you do not hear more frequent from me, but as I told you before it is only occasionally that an opportunity is afforded to send a letter. There is not any Post Offices on this side of the River. This has to be sent 15 miles to be mailed. I am mending a little every day, gaining strength. I suppose in the course of a few weeks I will be able to walk about by the help of cruthes [sic]. I am pretty positive that I will be at the Ferry in less than a week from now and then I can write to you and get an answer, or have you come to see me. Jennie, do not get uneasy about me. I am getting along as well as can be expected. I have as good attention paid me as any use in for any person to have.

I have not written to Father since I have been wounded. I thought it just as well if you would still let them know how I was. I rest very easy at night have very little pains, and have as good an appetite as any one need have for to stay in one room all the time. A Dixie lady says I shall give you her best compliments. She is one of those belonging to the place where I am at.

Remember me kindly to mother and aunt and the folks out at home. Tell them to give themselves no uneasiness about me, I am getting along smoothly.

Remember me kindly to all inquiring friends. Nothing more at this time but my Love to you while to this my name as your ever true devoted & affectionate

Husband.
Lt. John H. Black

* * *

Bolivar, Virginia
May 9, 1865
Dear Wife:

It is now just one week since I last wrote to you. I then stated that in less than a week from then I would be over the River. On Sunday last through the kindest of some of the best Union people to be found any where, I was brought to the Ferry, that is to Harpers Ferry, and from there I was taken to a Private house in Bolivar a mile from the Ferry. Mr. William Gore[34] is the name of the person I am staying with. It is the same place I boarded at when I was on duty at the Ferry last winter. I am very thankful that I have at last reached this place. I am as yet unable to walk. My feet are helpless, and are swollen nearly all the time. I rest very easy. Have not much pain. I heard from the Regiment since I came over the river. Sergt. Ginter came down from Winchester yesterday to see me. They had heard that morning that I was still among the living and had reached the Ferry. I also heard from you on yesterday. Mr. Williamson[35] of Co. "G" who taken prisoner on the same day I was wounded called to see me and stated the he had seen you on the 25th of April. Oh! but I was rejoiced to hear from you. It did me so much good.

Corporal James P. Stewart sent me all my letters that were on hand & other papers, and also, the receipt for the $270 that he sent you. I had thought that he had sent you $320 that I left with him, but he said after hearing that I was wounded & had fallen in the hands of the enemy, [he believed] that I would be robbed of every cent of money I had so he retained $50 for me and sent it to me yesterday.

True enough they did rob me to perfection. I had but $20 in money with me. They got that. Took my hat, Boots, Jacket, vest, shirt collar, letters, knife, comb, gold pen, and in fact everything but pantaloons, shirt, & drawers. While they were at that I made out to look on and say what I thought but there I was helpless. Since I have arrived here I have noticed an account of my death, in one of the papers of the Western part of Penna., But when I heard of it I did not believe it.

Well Jennie Dear I presume you have been wanting to come and see me but it was out of the question then. Here I am at the Ferry or near it and will not be able to take a trip home for some five or six weeks & maybe not so soon as that. I am told that it will require some five months altogether ere I will be able to walk around, and so you see my situation. If you feel like taking a trip to see me, ere I will be able to return home you will be a thousand times welcome in doing so. Just use your own discretion. If you come you will find a very nice place to stay at.

Remember me to Mother & Aunt and any others that may inquire about me.

My ever true devoted & undivided love to you. While my name to this as your ever true devoted and affectionate

Husband.

Lieut. John H. Black

Harpers Ferry, Va.

If you write address in care of William Gore.

* * *

Camp 12th PV Cav
May 29th 1865
Lt John H. Black
Dear friend:

I have Seen Dr Scholes [?] [word illegible] Md Director of this Post & they decided that D Kellogg at Harpers Ferry would be the proper officer to give a certificate for which you could get a proper Leave upon and D Scholes promises me he would Send to him to [words illegible] you could return [?] return and get him to Send the certificate to this place immediately, but further Said if you were ready to go home to leave at any time you choosed and your leave would be Sent to you &c. You are reported at these Hd Qrs absent Sick and will be So reported.

I have not seen the Q[uarter] M[aster] Sergt of Co "B."[36] He does not Stop in Camp but [I] will get his affadavit [sic] for you as Soon as I can get to See him, but your own affadavit will be Sufficient. All you will have to do is your case is to make an affadavit [sic] Stating the facts of your Case and that will relieve you of all responsibility. Your case is a very plain one. It would be [a] very unreasonable Idea to Suppose you would be held responsible for that property after the time you were wounded.

You would like to know how the new Layout is getting along. Well John the Lt Col[37] is all rite So far. [He] does very well but God Save us from the Majors[38] but the time will Soon [be] out. I think that we will all return to our peace full homes and be our own Cols & Majors &c.

John I wish you were here to enjoy the pleasures of receiving bows and Salutes from these grey backs that use[d] to boast & Brag of there Confederacy [?] & thinking that was captured in petticoat. They are very docile. John I cincerely hope that you will recover at least So you can walk as well as when you entered the Service. Any thing I can do for you will be done cheerfully. My Respects to Mrs Black &c. There are some of your lothes at Mrs Dunares [?] in Charlestown. They are in a Small Box, you can get them by Sending for them. Write me again Direct to Winchester. Matty Sends her respects to you &c.

> Yours very
> Respectfully
> P. H. McAteer
> Capt Co "G" 12 P Vols

* * *

Camp 12th Penna Cav
June 9. 65
Friend John:

I will employ a few of my leisure moments this evening in penning a few lines to you. I will enclose a letter that came here a few days ago for you and I thought I would pen a few lines and Send it along. I suppose that you have heard that the men of the Regt. whose time had expired prior to Oct. 1st have been Discharged and Some others. Poor Tom Ivory[39] Died at Salisbury N.C. Jan. 15 65. J[acob] Walters & Ch[ristian] Speece [?][40] have also turned up [illegible] all right. B. F. Stewart[41] Lew Fetters[42] & C. Fleck[43] have been Discharged. I tell you John it is bringing our Co. down a little. There is 18 men on Duty as Wagoners ambunance [sic] Drivers Cooks &c besides 8 (Eight) men on Daily Duty in the regt. This morning we have 28 Privates for Duty 3 Sergt. & 5 Corpls. It Seems queer to have such a Small amount of men in our company for Duty for you know we always had more men for Duty then any other Company in the Regt.

There is nothing of any importance going on here. They have Stopped Drilling for the time Being. There was Six companies Started up the Valley for Staunton under command of Maj Johnston [?] day before yesterday. Some Say they are going to Stay up there. I can not tell you for certain through. Another thing I can tell you it is awful hot here now and rain is needed very bad. I wish you were here with us for I feel Sorry for your Misfortune and I hope ere long you will be able to go about as of old. The Boys are all well and hearty. They complain a little of the Duty being hard but they go on Duty without mutch [sic] Bother or trouble.

Capt. [McAteer] is well and so is Lt. [McGough]. Ginter is also well and wishes to be remembered to you. I think I will close as I am about played out. You must Excuse this Scrawl for I have an awfull poor pen. I will now close wishing you all the Success you can have. I would be pleased to have an answer to this if it is convenient to you.

> I Remain with
> Respect Your
> Friend & Well Wisher
> Aaron Daugherty[44]
> Co. G. 12th Penna. Cav.
> Winchester, Virginia

* * *

Camp 12th PV Cav
June 15th 1865
Lieut John H. Black
Dr Sir

Your letter has been received and glad to hear that you have arrived Safe home, but Sorry that you had to go in the condition you are bit cincerely [*sic*] hope that you will get entirely well. You Speak of being mustered out of Service. I cannot tell you any thing definate [*sic*] in regard to that at present. There is an order here now to consolidate Regts immediately and muster out all Surpluss officers, but does not Say any thing in regard to disabled officers. I think if you get justice, you would be retained until the last. This is nothing to trouble you, you can just be as contented at home as if you were a citizen. You are reported absent Sick and will remain on the records of [the] Regt in that order until there are Some order[s] from higher authority, conflicting with it. I will let you know if any thing turns up that will interest you. Well John Soldiering has got to be a *drag*. We are all wornout laying around camp doing nothing, Sleep & eat is all. We are all broke. There is not ten dollars in the Regt that I know of. We will have on the first of the month Six months pay due us and no prospects of Pay master, So you can imagine how we put in the *time under the circumstances*.

There is a great scare on among Some of the officers of the Regt. There was a Roll Sent here yesterday to be filled up. It is the descriptive Roll and all officers that wish to be retained in Service have to file there [*sic*] intentions on this Roll and them that wants to go out will be mustered out immediately, but where the Laugh comes in all that file there [*sic*] intentions to Stop in the Service have to go before a board of *examination*. A good many of them *cant See it*, particularly them that *Col*

Reno has *marked* for he it is understood is one of the Board. I am going to Stand *the fire* how I will s[tand] [?] it cant Say nor to Speak [word obscured] and familiar to you I don't care a *dam*. I think after an officer has Served in the field four years he Should know his business well enough to go before any board and pass, but there are Some of the Smart ones of this Regt that will have to *get*. McGough is going out.[45] Well John I will dry up this institution for perhaps it will not be very interesting to you. If you want any information at any time let me know and all I know it will not take me long to tell you.

Give my kind regards to Mrs. Black &c. Matty [?] feels very proud that you mentioned her in your letter and Sends her complements to you &c. Write me on the recept. Of this. Give me all the news &c.

Your friend
P. H. McAteer
Capt Comdg Co "G"
12 Pa V Cav

* * *

Camp 12th Penna. Cav.
Near Winchester Va.
June 18, 1865
Friend John:

I will make an attempt to answer your letter which I received on last evening and was pleased to hear from you. Well I will now make an attemp[t] to give you a Small Sketch of our Proceedings Since I last wrote to you yesterday we moved our camp. We moved about three miles from Winchester towards Stevenson Depot but to the right of the Pike as you come out of Winchester. We will have a much better camp here after we get it fixed up a little. We are now in the woods. The most disadvantage is the water for the Horses which is a good ways off.

Well John they are Still Promoting officers I believe. I hear that Col. M. A. Reno has got the *Star* at last.[46] I will not say for certain but that is the report and I think it is pretty reliable to. There will be a great time here among the officers. Them that wants to Stay in the Service have to appear before the examining board. I hear that nearly all the officers of our Regiment are going out Except Some two or three. I believe Capt. McAteer is going to Stay well I Should be Sorry for to lose any of our officers now much more so now as they have been with us always and I do not want them to put any outsiders in to our company if it can be helped.

You talk about Resigning well you are free to think and do as you please but if I was in your Situation I would not Resign at this present time but I would hold my position till the Regiment was Discharged. You were good enough to fill the Place while you were well and in good health and I would hold on to it now as you are a cripple are [sic] was crippled in the Service of your country, and let others Say what they please that is my opinion. I was telling the Captain about it and he Said he thought you would be foolish to resign.

There is a great many of the Shoulder Straps put on *airs* but I hope there will be a time when Some people will be as good as others. There is a few of our own Regiment but [I] am happy to say none of our Company. There is no Difference in any of our officers. McAteer is just the Same as he always was and McGough is just the Same. Promotion did not make any difference on him but I suppose we will have a new Batch of officers if these old ones go out. I have not heard whether they will be Promoted out of the Regt. or whether they will put outsiders in. [I] hope they will not Shove outsiders in. As yet there is not mutch [sic] Sign of Discharging us Soon. I hope they will not keep us mutch longer for I tell you honestly I am more tired of Soldiering now than I ever was and this warm weather makes me not lazy but "*oh*" how tired. It is hot enough these [last] couple of Days to roast a Darkey. It is fairly Suffocating. I think if we had rain it would be Some cooler. The Boys are well and looking with eager eager eyes for an order to discharge the Vets. Ginter is well and wishes to be Remembered to you. Capt. & Lt. is also well. I think I will now close. Hoping to have an answer to this Soon.

I Remain Yours
With Respect
Aaron Daugherty
Co. G 12th Penna Cavalry
Winchester, Virginia

* * *

Little Orleans Md.
Dec. 14th 1865
John H. Black:
Dear Sir:

Although you did not reply to my last I feel anxious to hear from you. I heard by some means that you were wounded last spring and that you had recovered.

I was in Martinsburg last week and seen Mr. Ross and he told me that he thought that you did not recover which I was very sorry to hear. Rumours are not to be depended on so I have concluded to write again to see if I cant reach you.

If you have suffered from wounds be assured that you have my Earnest sympathy. I am of opinion and hope that you had the good luck to get home, and that you now enjoy the comforts of home and society.

I have a son that is four months old. He is a fine large boy and think that he will make a soldier by the time that we will have to thrash the rebels again.

When we held our Elections here, it was a sorrowful time to rebels. They had no show [and] they found it best to take a stand off. There is nothing transpiring here consequently there is no news of importance stirring. My health is not very good. I am at times very painful with Rheumatism.

If you did collect that note send me the money and if not send the note and I will send it to Maj. Payne and get him to collect it for me. Give my regards to all inquiring friends in particular to your Father.

Your companion in arms,
Wm. J. Blackmund [?][47]

Address Little Orleans
    Alleghany Co. Md.

Chapter 6

Postwar Years

Despite the seriousness of his Civil War wounds, John Black lived for nearly sixty years after the conflict. He was able to maintain a relatively active lifestyle, although his physical problems greatly affected him. Returning to his prewar occupation, Black taught in the Duncansville school system for several years after the war, and he and Jennie lived in her family home in Duncansville. He was offered the position of county school superintendent but declined due to his poor health. Black later taught in Allegheny township. While the 1880 federal census listed his occupation as teacher, it also listed him in the category of those who were "maimed, crippled, bedridden or otherwise disabled."[1]

In politics, Black remained an "ardent Republican," as did most Union war veterans. Upon his death, it was noted that Black "voted for every Republican president after Fillmore to the present." In 1866 he was elected to the position of county treasurer, serving three years. He did not, however, seek further political office. Black also participated in veterans' affairs. He regularly attended Memorial Day observances and "never failed to enthuse the attendants at the services with an inspiring address." Later in his life, a Sons of Union Veterans camp was organized in Duncansville and named the Captain [sic] John H. Black Camp 224 in his honor.[2]

As he aged, Black's war wound continued to impact his health. Later in life, it was reported that the old veteran "is obliged to remain in-doors the greater part of his time, and much of this time he is obliged to spend in his bed. . . . If he remains out of his bed for an hour, his feet become very much swollen, causing him increased pain."[3]

Until her death in 1908, Jennie cared for her husband. She administered pain relief medication to him "four to six times a day and frequently oftener." A private servant was hired by the family to do housework so Mrs. Black could concentrate on nursing her husband. Jennie felt "obliged to keep an almost constant watch" over John. Frequently he was "attacked with nervous spells which come without warning."[4]

John Black initially received a monthly pension from the federal government of $17.00, which was later increased to $20.00 and then to $31.25. In June 1878 he asked for an increase in his stipend to $50.00. After this appeal was rejected by the Pension Bureau, Black enlisted the aid of the House of Representatives' Committee on Invalid Pensions, which voted to support a bill to increase the veteran's pension accordingly. Doctor George W. Smith examined Black for the committee. His report gives a detailed description of Black's physical condition:

> I found him to have a gunshot wound of his spine. Ball entered the fourth vertebra (lumba), remaining there yet. He was partially paralyzed in both his legs and almost complete paralysis of both feet. I commenced to treat him about 1866. I have visited and prescribed for him at intervals ever since, using *excito-motor* stimulants, tonics, both general and local, the electric current, and all the modern treatment and appliances. For years he could manage to get about and teach school at times, but has gradually grown more paralyzed. The paralysis is progressive. The bladder and rectum are involved, and for more than one year [he] has not been able to attend to his personal wants and comforts, and has to have other persons to assist him. He is helpless and permanently disabled from the above-named wound, and from his present condition it is my opinion that he is not safe to be left entirely alone for one moment.[5]

In June 1880, H.R. 2862 was approved, granting Black an increase in his pension to fifty dollars.

Black's condition further deteriorated in his later years. On April 11, 1908, Jennie, his devoted wife of forty-four years, died after "an illness of two weeks' duration." Her obituary noted, "The deceased had not been in good health for some time, but not one surmised the end was so near or that her illness was of a serious nature. She was born, reared, married and lived all her life in the house where now lie her mortal remains." It added, "She was a devoted member of the Methodist church all her life. She was of a remarkably affectionate, sympathetic . . . and charitable nature."[6] The couple had no children of their own, perhaps as a result of John Black's war wounds. They did, however, adopt two children, Carrie and Lillian. The former cared for her father after Jennie Black's death.

In 1920, Black asked the Pension Bureau for another increase in his stipend, noting that he was unable to move about without the aid of a wheelchair. John Barton Payne of the bureau replied that, under existing laws, Black could not receive a pension increase for disability to both of his legs or feet. If, Payne stated, Black had a disability of one hand and one foot, he would then be entitled to additional compensation. Had the old veteran's condition not been so serious, he might have seen humor in the government's peculiar gradations for disability.[7]

On May 10, 1922, eighty-seven-year-old John H. Black finally succumbed to his wounds and advancing age. His final illness was listed as cerebral apoplexy, but this death certificate could have easily stated "Mortally Wounded at Hamilton, Virginia, March 21, 1865—Died Duncansville, Pennsylvania, May 10, 1922."

Funeral services for Black were held at the Hicks Memorial Methodist Church in Duncansville. Members of the John H. Black Camp 224 served as pallbearers during the services. The veteran was interred in the Carson Valley Cemetery next to his beloved Jennie. Several local newspapers carried obituaries on Black's death, one noting that, following his wounding in 1865, the *Hollidaysburg Register* had printed a notice that Black had been killed. Black carried the faded clipping with him until his actual death fifty-seven years later.[8]

Appendix

Service of the Twelfth Pennsylvania Cavalry

Organization

Organized at Philadelphia, December 1861 to April 1862

Ordered to Washington, D.C., April 1862

Attached to the Military District of Washington until September 1862

Fourth Brigade, Pleasanton's Cavalry Division, Army of the Potomac, until October 1862

Averill's Cavalry Command, Eighth Army Corps, Middle Department, until November 1862

Defended the upper Potomac, Eighth Corps, until February 1863

Adapted from Dyer, *A Compendium of the War of the Rebellion* 2: 1563–64.

First Brigade, Second Division, Eighth Corps, until June 1863

Pierce's Brigade, Department of the Susquehanna, until July 1863

McReynold's Command, Department of the Susquehanna, until August 1863

Service

Duty at Washington, D.C., until June 20, 1862

Moved to Manassas Junction, Virginia, and guarded the Orange and Alexander Railroad until August

Moved to Bristoe and thence to Alexandria; picketed the north bank of the Potomac from Chain Bridge to Edward's Ferry until September

Maryland campaign, September to October

Frederick, Maryland, September 12

Battle of Antietam, Maryland, September 16–17

Assigned to duty on a line of the Baltimore and Ohio Railroad, headquarters at Sir John's Run, Bath, (West) Virginia

Martinsburg, November 6

Moorefield, November 9

Newtown, November 24

Kearneysville, December 26

Bunker Hill, January 1, 1863

Near Smithfield and Charles Town, February 12

Mill Wood Road near Winchester, April 8

Reconnaissance from Winchester to Wardensville and Strasburg, April 20

Operations in the Shenandoah Valley, April 22–29

Strasburg Road, Fisher's Hill, April 22

Scout to Strasburg, April 25–30

Cedarville and Winchester, June 12

Winchester, June 13–15

McConnellsburg, Pennsylvania, June 24

Cunningham's Cross Roads, Pennsylvania, July 5

Greencastle, Pennsylvania, July 5 (detachment)

Near Clear Springs, Maryland, July 10

Moved to Sharpsburg, Maryland, and thence to Martinsburg, August 3; duty there until July 1864

Jeffersonton, October 10, 1863

Near Winchester, February 5, 1864

Middletown, February 6

Winchester, April 26

Affair in Loudoun County, June 9 (detachment)

Charles Town and Duffield Station (or Duffield's Depot), June 29

Bolivar Heights, July 2

Near Hillsboro, July 15–16

Charles Town, July 17

Snicker's Ferry, July 17–18

Ashby's Gap and Berry's Ford, July 19

Near Kernstown, July 23

Winchester, July 24

Bunker Hill and Martinsburg, July 25

Cherry Run, July 28

Winchester, July 29

Guard and garrison duty at Charles Town, covering the railroad from Harpers Ferry to Winchester until March 1865

Charles Town, September 27, 1864

Halltown, November 12

Mount Zion Church, November 12

Newtown, November 24

Charles Town, November 29 (detachment)

Affair at Harpers Ferry, February 3, 1865 (detachment)

Scout from Harpers Ferry into Loudoun County, March 20–23

Near Hamilton, March 21

Goose Creek, March 23

Duty at Winchester and in the Shenandoah Valley until July

Mustered out July 20, 1865

Regiment lost during service 2 officers and 32 enlisted men killed and mortally wounded and 1 officer and 107 enlisted men by disease. Total 142.

Notes

Preface

1. Unidentified newspaper clipping with John H. Black obituary, private collection of Marguerite Campbell, Claysburg, Pa.; Jesse C. Sell, *Twentieth Century History of Altoona and Blair County, Pennsylvania and Representative Citizens* (Chicago: Richmond-Arnold, 1911), 657–58; 1850 and 1860 federal census, Blair County, Pa., National Archives and Record Administration, Washington, D.C. (hereafter cited as NARA).

2. See Sell, *Twentieth Century History;* and J. Simpson Africa, *History of Huntingdon and Blair Counties, Pennsylvania* (n.p., n.d.) for general histories of the county.

3. 1860 federal census, Blair County, Pa.

4. David S. Heidler and Jeanne T. Heidler, eds., *Encyclopedia of the American Civil War: A Political , Social, and Military History* (New York: W. W. Norton, 2000), 1485–86; Walter Licht, "Civil Wars, 1850–1900," in *Pennsylvania: A History of the Commonwealth,* ed. Randall M. Miller and William Pencak (University Park: Pennsylvania State Univ. Press, 2002), 203–55; Wayland Fuller Dunaway, *A History of Pennsylvania* (New York: Prentice-Hall, 1935), 493–523. A more modern, specialized study of the state during the war years is William Blair and William Pencak, eds.,

Making and Remaking Pennsylvania's Civil War (University Park: Pennsylvania State Univ. Press, 2001).

5. Larry D. Smith, *150th Anniversary History of Blair County, Pennsylvania* (Apollo, Pa.: Closson Press, 1997), 190–201. Floyd G. Hoenstine, *Military Services and Genealogical Records of Soldiers of Blair County, Pennsylvania* (Harrisburg, Pa.: Telegraph Press, 1940) contains a complete roster of the county's Civil War veterans. See also William B. Hesseltine, *Lincoln and the War Governors* (New York: Alfred A. Knopf, 1948).

6. Sell, *Twentieth Century History*, 657–58.

7. John H. Black to Jennie Leighty, July 5, 1862, John H. Black Collection, photocopies, private collection of David Coles, Farmville, Va. Unless otherwise noted, all subsequent Black letters are from this collection.

8. Ibid.

9. Ibid.

10. Ibid., July 24, 1862.

11. Ibid., Nov. 17, 1863.

12. Ibid., June 12, 1862.

13. Ibid., Sept. 27, 1862.

14. Ibid., Dec. 13, 1863.

15. Ibid., June 20, 1862.

16. Ibid., Oct. 30, 1864.

17. Ibid., Dec. 28, 1864.

18. *Altoona Mirror,* Apr. 11, 1908; 1850 and 1860 federal censuses, Blair County, Pa.

19. Black to Leighty, May 31, 1862.

20. Ibid., Mar. 22, 1863.

21. Ibid., Oct. 20, 1863.

22. Several works highlight these themes. See, for example, Karen Lystra, *Searching the Heart: Women, Men, and Romantic Love in Nineteenth-Century America* (New York: Oxford Univ. Press, 1989); Anthony Rotundo, *American Manhood: Transformations in Masculinity from the Revolution to the Modern Era* (New York: Harper Collins, 1993); Reid Mitchell, *The Vacant Chair: The Northern Soldier Leaves Home* (New York: Oxford Univ. Press, 1993); and Drew Gilpin Faust, *This Republic of Suffering: Death and the American Civil War* (New York: Alfred A. Knopf, 2008).

23. Black to Leighty, Jan. 3, 1864.

24. Black to Jennie Black, Dec. 8, 1864.

25. Black to Black, May 6, 1864.

26. On guerrillas, see Michael Fellman, *Inside War: The Guerrilla Conflict in Missouri During the American Civil War* (New York: Oxford Univ. Press, 1989); Robert R. Mackey, *The Uncivil War: Irregular Warfare in the Upper South, 1861–1865* (Norman: Univ. of Oklahoma Press, 2004); and Daniel E. Sutherland, *A Savage Conflict: The Decisive Role of Guerrillas in the American Civil War* (Chapel Hill: Univ. of North Carolina Press, 2009).

27. There are many modern works that deal with the motivation and the experiences of Civil War soldiers. Among the most helpful are James McPherson, *For Cause and Comrades: Why Men Fought in the Civil War* (New York: Oxford Univ. Press, 1997); Reid Mitchell, *Civil War Soldiers: Their Expectations and Their Experiences* (New York: Viking Penguin, 1998); Randall Jimerson, *The Private Civil War: Popular Thought During the Sectional Conflict* (Baton Rouge: Louisiana State Univ. Press, 1998); Dora L. Costa and Matthew E. Kahn, *Heroes and Cowards: The Social Face of War* (Princeton, N.J.: Princeton Univ. Press, 2008); and Larry B. Maier, *Leather and Steel: The 12th Pennsylvania Cavalry in the Civil War* (Shippensburg, Pa.: Burd Street Press, 2001).

Chapter 1

1. Samuel P. Bates, *Pennsylvania Volunteers, 1861–65*, 5 vols. (Harrisburg, Pa.: B. Singerly, 1869–71), vol. 1:134–35, 140. Subsequent references to specific soldiers have been taken primarily from information contained from the printed rosters in this publication.

2. Ibid. See also Hoenstine, *Military Services and Genealogical Records,* passim; and Frederick H. Dyer, *A Compendium of the War of the Rebellion,* 2 vols. (reprint, Dayton, Ohio: Press of Morningside Bookshop, 1978), vol. 2:1583.

3. Dyer, *Compendium* 2:1583.

4. James McPherson, *Battle Cry of Freedom: The Civil War Era* (New York: Oxford Univ. Press, 1988), 334–50, provides an overview of the Manassas campaign; Bates, *Pennsylvania Volunteers* 1:134–35.

5. Identity unknown. Toole apparently was a Pennsylvania acquaintance of John and Jennie. There are several Ellen Tooles listed in the 1860 federal census for Pennsylvania, but the only adult resided in Philadelphia's Second Ward. 1860 federal census, Philadelphia, Pa.

6. Identity unknown. There were seven men with the Christian name of James in Company H alone. Bates, *Pennsylvania Volunteers* 3:140.

7. Col. John W. Johnston of Youngstown was colonel of the Fourteenth Pennsylvania Infantry. He had seen previous military service in the Mexican War. Bates, *Pennsylvania Volunteers* 3:134–35.

8. The identities of "Skyles" and "Louiza" (or "Lue"), who are referred to frequently in Black's subsequent letters, remain somewhat mysterious. Lue was either a friend or relative of Jennie, while Skyles was Lue's sweetheart. His hesitancy to join the service was a constant source of aggravation for John Black, though evidently he finally did enlist in late 1862. There are no men with the surname Skyles listed in the most recent roster of Union soldiers from Pennsylvania, though there are fourteen men with the surname Skiles. See Janet B. Hewett, ed., *Roster of Union Soldiers, 1861–1865*, 33 vols. (Wilmington, N.C.: Broadfoot, 1997–2001), vol. 3:475. This thirty-three-volume set is arranged by state, though not consecutively numbered. There are four volumes of Pennsylvania soldiers, and this and all subsequent references refer to these volumes. The older Bates roster, however, lists two men with the surname Skyles in the Fourteenth Pennsylvania Cavalry. The most likely individual is Henry Skyles, who was mustered into Company L on November 14, 1862, and transferred to Company E on July 31, 1865. He was promoted to corporal in August 1865 and mustered out of service late the same month. The second soldier is Private Archibald Skyles, who was mustered into Company F, Fourteenth Pennsylvania Cavalry on November 23, 1862, and deserted in June 1863. See Bates, *Pennsylvania Volunteers* 4:873, 879, 891.

   Henry Skiles/Skyles was born on October 15, 1834, in Pennsylvania, and he appears in the 1850 federal census as a fifteen-year-old schoolboy living in Allegheny County with his parents James and Catharine Skyles and two brothers. According to census records, Skyles married Luella Boli (born June 1832, died 1922, and also listed variously with a first name of Kate, Katherine, or Catharine) in February 1858. In 1860 the couple lived in Allegheny County with their two-month-old son William. Henry Skyles was a farmer with a personal estate valued at $200.00. After the war he and Luella had four additional children. He applied for a pension in 1890 and died in Sewickley, Pennsylvania, on April 15, 1929. The problem with this identification is that Henry and Luella evidently were married prior to the war and had a child in 1860, and Black's letters indicate that Skyles and Lue were courting but not married. While it appears likely that Henry Skiles/Skyles and Luella Boli are the individuals referred to as "Skyles" and "Lue" in John Black's letters, this has not been determined conclusively. See the 1850, 1860, 1870, and 1900 federal censuses, Allegheny County, Pa.; U.S. Civil War Soldier Records and Profiles, Ancestry.com, http://www.ancestry.com/; Luella Katherine Boli Overview, Ancestry.com, http://www.ancestry.com/.

9. Jennie's mother was Sophia Walters Leighty, who was born in 1810 in Ebensburg, Cambria County, Pennsylvania. She married George Leighty, and had two children, William, who was born in 1829 and died in 1898, and Susan Jane (Jennie), who was born in 1837 and died in 1908. It is assumed that George Leighty died prior to 1850, as he cannot be identified in cen-

sus records for those years. In 1850 Sophia Leighty lived in Blair County with William and Jennie and with thirty-five-year-old Susannah Walters. In 1860, she and Jennie lived together at Newry in Blair County, and in 1870 she was living with John and Jennie Black. Sophia Leighty Overview, Ancestry.com, http://www.ancestry.com/; 1850, 1860, and 1870 federal censuses, Blair County, Pa.

10. Thomas Holland was mustered into service for three months on April 24, 1861, and was discharged upon the mustering out of the regiment. Holland was born in 1821 and died in 1902. He is buried in St. Patrick's Cemetery in Newry. Bates, *Pennsylvania Volunteers* 1:140; Hoenstine, *Military Services and Genealogical Records*, 207.

Chapter 2

1. Compiled Service Record of John H. Black and Pension File of John H. Black, NARA.

2. Ibid.; Bates, *Pennsylvania Volunteers* 3:1143; Frank H. Taylor, *Philadelphia in the Civil War, 1861–1865* (Philadelphia: Published by the City, 1913), 170–71; Hoenstine, *Military Services and Genealogical Records*, 127–28; Maier, *Leather and Steel*, 1–15.

3. Maier, *Leather and Steel*, 8–12, 16–21.

4. Bates, *Pennsylvania Volunteers* 3:1143. See also Charles Weirick to sister, June 7, 1862, Charles Weirick Collection, United States Army History Institute, Carlisle Barracks, Pa. Weirick served in Company F of the Twelfth Cavalry.

5. Samuel O. Evans served in Company G of the Twelfth Cavalry. He was mustered into service on January 8, 1862, for three years, and was discharged on February 17, 1865, at the expiration of his term. According to John Black's letter of March 12, 1865, Evans was later commissioned a lieutenant in the Sixteenth Pennsylvania Cavalry, although his name does not appear in the published roster of the Sixteenth Cavalry. Bates, *Pennsylvania Volunteers* 3:1166.

6. Jacob Walters served in Company G of the Twelfth Cavalry. He was mustered into service on January 8, 1862, for three years, and was discharged by general order on June 5, 1865. He was captured by Confederate forces on June 29, 1864, and briefly imprisoned. Walters was perhaps a relative of Jennie, as her mother's maiden name was Walters. Bates, *Pennsylvania Volunteers* 3:168.

7. Barney Engle served in Company G of the Twelfth Cavalry. He was mustered into service on January 8, 1862, for three years and mustered out on July 20, 1865, having previously reenlisted as a Veteran Volunteer. Bates, *Pennsylvania Volunteers* 3:1166.

8. Probably James M. Irvine, Company M, Twelfth Pennsylvania Cavalry. Irvine was mustered into service on February 21, 1862, for three years and mustered out on July 20, 1865, having previously reenlisted as a Veteran Volunteer. Bates, *Pennsylvania Volunteers* 3:1179.

9. Perhaps Susannah Walters, who lived with Jennie's family at the time of the 1850 federal census. Evidently she was a relative (perhaps Jennie's aunt), as Walters was the maiden name of Jennie's mother. 1850 federal census, Blair County, Pa.

10. William Frishmuth of Philadelphia was authorized by President Lincoln on November 5, 1861, to organize a cavalry regiment. He apparently was never formally mustered into service, and he resigned on April 20, 1862. Lt. Col. Lewis B. Pierce was promoted to colonel on April 23, 1862, as a replacement for Frishmuth. Bates, *Pennsylvania Volunteers* 3:1142, 1148; Maier, *Leather and Steel,* 1–3.

11. "Varioloid" is described as a "mild form of smallpox, suffered by persons who previously had smallpox or who had been vaccinated." Glenna R. Schroeder-Lein, *The Encyclopedia of Civil War Medicine* (Armonk, N.Y.: M.E. Sharpe, 2008), 321.

12. Col. Elmer Ephraim Ellsworth was the first Northern martyr of the war. A friend of Abraham Lincoln, Ellsworth organized the New York Fire Zouaves, which he led into Alexandria, Virginia, on May 24, 1861. After tearing down a Confederate flag that had been flying over the Marshall House Hotel, Ellsworth was shot and killed by the secessionist proprietor, James Jackson. Heidler and Heidler, *Encyclopedia of the American Civil War* 2:647.

13. Nothing specific is known about Black's relationship with these men, though at the time of the 1860 federal census, he resided in the household of a merchant named James McIntosh. 1860 federal census, Blair County, Pa.

14. Jacob Kohler was mustered into service as major of the Twelfth Pennsylvania Cavalry on March 6, 1862, to serve for three years. He was promoted to lieutenant colonel on April 28, 1862, and was discharged on October 17, 1862. The published roster of the Twelfth Cavalry provides no additional information on the accidental shootings mentioned by Black (Bates, *Pennsylvania Volunteers* 3:1148), but Maier's history of the regiment does. According to that source, an intoxicated Kohler, angry that some of the men had refused to move when the regiment left Washington, threatened to fire into one group before being restrained by another officer, but he then rode on to another part of the regiment and fired into a group, "wounding 3 innocent men." Maier, *Leather and Steel,* 20–21.

15. The letter that Black mentions in not in the John H. Black Collection.

16. Sangster's Station was located on the Orange and Alexandria Railroad, southeast of Centerville, Virginia.

17. Site of the first major battle of the war, fought on July 21, 1861. First Bull Run, or First Manassas as it was known in the South, was a major Confederate victory. David J. Eicher, *The Longest Night: A Military History of the Civil War* (New York: Simon Schuster, 2001), 87–101.

18. David Gardner of Blair County was mustered into Company G of the First Pennsylvania Cavalry as first lieutenant on September 27, 1861. He was subsequently promoted to captain, major, and lieutenant colonel and was mustered out in September 1864. Henry C. Beamer was mustered into the First Pennsylvania Cavalry in August 1861. He was promoted to sergeant major, first lieutenant, and captain and resigned his commission on April 12, 1863. Bates, *Pennsylvania Volunteers* 1:1025–26, 1041.

19. Irvin McDowell (1818–1885) had commanded the Union forces at First Bull Run in July 1861. After the defeat he remained in Virginia commanding successively a corps in the Army of the Potomac, the Army of the Rappahannock, and the Third Corps in the Army of Virginia. He was criticized for his service in the Second Bull Run campaign of July–August 1862 and relieved from command. McDowell later commanded the Department of the Pacific. See Ezra J. Warner, *Generals in Blue: Lives of Union Commanders* (Baton Rouge: Louisiana State Univ. Press, 1964), 297–99. Earl Schenck Miers, *Lincoln Day by Day: A Chronology, 1809–1865*, 3 vols. in 1 (Dayton, Ohio: Morningside House, 1991), vol. 3:122, records that the president "accompanied by Sec. Stanton and Gen. Wadsworth, reviews Scott Cavalry Regiment." The source does not indicate the location of the review.

20. 1st Lt. Thad S. Shannon was mustered into service on February 17, 1862, for three years. He resigned from the service on June 25, 1862. Bates, *Pennsylvania Volunteers* 3:1165.

21. Milton Funk was mustered into service as a private in Company G, Twelfth Pennsylvania Cavalry on January 8, 1862. He was never promoted to first lieutenant in Company G, as John Black wrote, but was transferred to Company C on November 10, 1862, and promoted to second lieutenant. Funk was killed in action at Winchester, Virginia, on July 24, 1864. Bates, *Pennsylvania Volunteers* 3:155, 1167.

22. The captain of Company G was Adam Hartman, mustered in on February 17, 1862, and discharged on July 21, 1863. It is unclear which lieutenant Black was referring to. Bates, *Pennsylvania Volunteers* 3:1165.

23. The "Upper Ten" was a term that originated in the 1850s to describe the social elite in major cities. John Russell Bartlett, *Dictionary of Americanisms,* 2nd ed. (Boston: Little, Brown, 1859), 494.

24. Black was writing about the Peninsula campaign, Maj. Gen. George B. McClellan's attempt to capture Richmond during the early summer of 1862. See Stephen W. Sears, *To the Gates of Richmond: The Peninsula*

Campaign (New York: Ticknor and Fields, 1992) for the best survey of this campaign.

25. One history of the Twelfth Cavalry notes that "it was past the middle of July before the command was mounted, and little progress had been made in training and discipline, before active operations commenced." Bates, *Pennsylvania Volunteers* 3:1143. See also Maier, *Leather and Steel,* 26–28, for another account of the regiment receiving its mounts.

26. In the summer of 1862, President Lincoln called for a new quota of enlistees to put down the rebellion. The Confederate surge in the Shenandoah Valley under Gen. Thomas J. "Stonewall" Jackson alarmed Washington into calling on the Northern governors for additional troops. See Hesseltine, *Lincoln and the War Governors,* 194–95; Roy P. Basler, ed., *The Collected Works of Abraham Lincoln,* 8 vols. (New Brunswick, N.J.: Rutgers Univ. Press, 1953), vol. 5:296–97.

27. Henry Engle was mustered into service in Company G on January 8, 1862, for three years. He died in Annapolis, Maryland, on August 12, 1863. Bates, *Pennsylvania Volunteers* 3:1166. The entry in Bates makes no mention of Engle being absent without permission.

28. John Black was referring to the new Pennsylvania regiments raised under President Lincoln's new call for troops.

29. A James Hammer served in Company G of the 175th Infantry (Drafted Militia), and a James H. Hammer in Company I of the Thirty-third Militia (emergency 1863). In a subsequent letter, Black mentions Hammer as serving in a company of Blair County Militia. Hewett, *Roster of Union Soldiers* 2:135.

30. There is no listing for Mollie Slayman found in the 1860 federal census for Pennsylvania.

31. *The War of the Rebellion: A Compilation of the Official Records of the Union and Confederate Armies* (Washington, D.C.: Government Printing Office, 1880–1901), ser. 1, vol. 12, pt. 2, p. 670 (cited hereafter as OR with appropriate series, volume, and part numbers); Maier, *Leather and Steel,* 26–43; Bates, *Pennsylvania Volunteers* 3:1143–44; and Taylor, *Philadelphia in the Civil War,* 170–71.

32. "Determined" quote from Bates, *Pennsylvania Volunteers* 3:1144; "alternative" quote from Taylor, *Philadelphia in the Civil War,* 170. See also Maier, *Leather and Steel,* 31–43; Edward J. Stackpole, *From Cedar Mountain to Antietam* (Harrisburg, Pa.: Stackpole, 1959); John J. Hennessy, *Return to Bull Run: The Campaign and Battle of Second Manassas* (New York: Simon & Schuster, 1993); and *Philadelphia Inquirer,* Aug. 30, Sept. 1, 1862.

33. Bates, *Pennsylvania Volunteers* 3:1143–44; also OR, ser. 1, vol. 12, pt. 3:692, 695–96, 722, 753, 790; and Maier, *Leather and Steel,* 31–43.

34. Pension File of John H. Black and Compiled Service Record of John H. Black. Camp Parole in Annapolis, Maryland, was one of three camps established to accept paroled Union prisoners of war until exchanged for Southern prisoners; see Heidler and Heidler, *Encyclopedia of the American Civil War* 3:1566–69; and Charles W. Sanders, *While in the Hands of the Enemy: Military Prisons of the Civil War* (Baton Rouge: Louisiana State Univ. Press, 2005), which has the best overview of the exchange/parole system.

35. William W. Gwin had not been killed. He was mustered into service in Company G on February 14, 1862, and discharged on February 17, 1865; see Bates, *Pennsylvania Volunteers* 3:1167. George Vaughn, a twenty-two-year-old brick maker from Duncansville, served with John Black in Company H of the three-month Fourteenth Pennsylvania Infantry in 1861. He subsequently enlisted in August 1862 in Company A, 125th Pennsylvania Infantry, a nine-month regiment. Vaughn was severely wounded in the leg at Antietam in September 1862 and was discharged due to disability on April 1, 1863. Regimental Committee, *History of the One Hundred and Twenty-fifth Regiment Pennsylvania Volunteers, 1862–1863* (Philadelphia: J. B. Lippincott, 1906), 86, 297.

36. Reeves is unidentified.

37. Private William K. Hollis was mustered into service on February 12, 1862, for three years and was discharged by special order on November 20, 1865. He had previously reenlisted as a Veteran Volunteer. Bates, *Pennsylvania Volunteers* 3:1167.

38. No Richard Yost is listed in the published roster of Company G, Twelfth Pennsylvania Cavalry.

39. Private Patrick Byrne was mustered into service on February 14, 1862, for three years' service, and was mustered out with his company on July 20, 1865. He had previously reenlisted as a Veteran Volunteer. Bates, *Pennsylvania Volunteers* 3:1166.

40. Sergeant Matthew Aiken was mustered into service on January 8, 1862, for three years and was mustered out with his company on July 20, 1865. He had previously reenlisted as a Veteran Volunteer. Bates, *Pennsylvania Volunteers* 3:1166.

41. Private James Funk was mustered into service on February 18, 1862, for three years and was discharged upon expiration of his term of service on February 17, 1865. Bates, *Pennsylvania Volunteers* 3:1166.

42. Following the Second Bull Run debacle of August 1862, General McClellan was again appointed to command the Army of the Potomac and led it to Sharpsburg, Maryland, where on September 17 his army fought Gen. Robert E. Lee's Army of Northern Virginia. See Eicher, *Longest Night*,

347–66; and Mark M. Boatner III, *The Civil War Dictionary* (New York: David McKay, 1959), 17–21.

43. Although Confederate prisoners of war would later be paroled to fight Indians in the West, there was never a serious effort to use Union parolees in a similar manner. On the galvanized Yankees, see Heidler and Heidler, *Encyclopedia of the American Civil War* 2: 803; see also Dee Brown, *The Galvanized Yankees* (Lincoln: Univ. of Nebraska Press, 1986).

44. Pvt. William McCaulley was mustered into service on February 5, 1862, for three years and was mustered out with his company on July 20, 1865, having previously reenlisted as a Veteran Volunteer. John Black had received erroneous information concerning McCaulley's death. Bates, *Pennsylvania Volunteers* 3:1167.

45. Pvt. John Lehr was mustered into service on January 8, 1862, for three years. He is not listed on the unit's muster-out roll. Bates, *Pennsylvania Volunteers* 3:1166.

46. Pvt. Thomas Brannan was mustered into service on February 5, 1862, for three years. He is not shown on the unit's muster-out roll. Bates, *Pennsylvania Volunteers* 3: 1166.

47. Pvt. George Bub of Company E is listed as dying on October 21, 1862, and buried in the National Cemetery at Sharpsburg, Maryland. No other Company E soldier is shown to have died around this time. Bates, *Pennsylvania Volunteers* 3:1166.

48. The *Oxford English Dictionary* defines this term as "a slang phrase implying that the words to which it is appended express the reverse of what is really meant." It is also described as "light and playful sarcasm." *Oxford English Dictionary*, 2nd. ed., 1989, http://dictionary.oed.com/.

49. Sutlers were private businessmen who followed Civil War armies, selling goods and foodstuffs normally not available to private soldiers, although usually at an inflated price; see Francis Lord, *Civil War Sutlers and Their Wares* (New York: T. Yoseloff, 1969).

50. The Soldier's Retreat served food and provided shelter for servicemen passing through the capital. It was located near the Washington railroad depot. See Matthew Pinsker, *Lincoln's Sanctuary: Abraham Lincoln and the Soldier's Home* (New York: Oxford Univ. Press, 2005); Ernest B. Furgurson, *Freedom Rising: Washington in the Civil War* (New York: Alfred A. Knopf, 2004); and Margaret Leech, *Reveille in Washington, 1860–1865* (New York: Harper & Brothers, 1941), 172–86, 196.

51. Black was probably referring to either Adam Hartman, the original commander of Company G, or Patrick H. McAteer, who was mustered into service on February 17, 1862, as a first lieutenant and promoted to captain on December 22, 1863. Bates, *Pennsylvania Volunteers* 3:1165.

Chapter 3

1. Bates, *Pennsylvania Volunteers* 3:1144–46. See also Pension File of John H. Black and Compiled Service Record of John H. Black.

2. Kearneysville, West Virginia, was located on the Baltimore and Ohio Railroad, southwest of Shepherdstown and northwest of Charles Town.

3. Perhaps William Bartley (b. 1832), who in 1860 was residing in Altoona's East Ward. 1860 federal census for Pennsylvania.

4. Unidentified. There is a David Leighty living in Blair County and another in Fayette County in the 1860 census. 1860 federal census, Blair County and Fayette County, Pa.

5. Slayman was apparently a friend of John and Jennie who served in another Pennsylvania regiment. Perhaps he is related to the Mollie Slayman mentioned in a previous letter. A George W. Slayman served in Companies D and I of the 137th Pennsylvania Infantry. Hewett, *Roster of Union Soldiers* 3:477.

6. Stan Cohen, *The Civil War in West Virginia: A Pictorial History* (Charleston, W.Va.: Pictorial Histories, 1981), 105–6; *OR*, ser. 1, vol. 15, pt. 2:347, 349–50, 298–399, 436, 454–55, 496. Evidence of the dilapidated condition of the Twelfth Regiment at this time can be found on page 436 of the latter source, where Brig. Gen. B. S. Roberts states, "It is folly to call the Twelfth Pennsylvania Regiment Cavalry. They have but 320 men, and their colonel informed me that 20 of his horses could not get up yesterday."

7. *OR*, ser. 1, vol. 13, pt. 1:96–97, 138, 144–45; and Maier, *Leather and Steel*, 72–75.

8. The best scholarly study of the Gettysburg campaign, which also includes a brief summary of the Battle of Winchester, remains Edwin B. Coddington, *The Gettysburg Campaign: A Study in Command* (New York: Charles Scribner's Sons, 1968). See particularly 84–90, quote from 87. A more detailed study of the campaign's opening stages, though somewhat dated, is Wilbur S. Nye, *Here Come the Rebels* (Baton Rouge: Louisiana State Univ. Press, 1965), 66–123. The relevant battle reports are in *OR*, ser. 1, vol. 27, pts. 1–3. On the Second Battle of Winchester, see Richard Duncan, *Beleaguered Winchester: A Virginia Community at War, 1861–1865* (Baton Rouge: Louisiana State Univ. Press, 2007); Larry B. Maier, *Gateway to Gettysburg: The Second Battle of Winchester* (Shippensburg, Pa.: White Mane, 2002), 101–280; Maier, *Leather and Steel*, 77–102; and Charles S. Grunder and Brandon H. Beck, *The Second Battle of Winchester, June 12–15, 1863* (Lynchburg, Va.: H. E. Howard, Inc., 1989), 8–65.

9. Bates, *Pennsylvania Volunteers* 3:1144–45; Maier, *Leather and Steel*, 77–102; Maier, *Gateway to Gettysburg*, 101–280.

10. Bates, *Pennsylvania Volunteers* 3:1144–45; and Maier, *Leather and Steel,* 77–102; Maier, *Gateway to Gettysburg,* 101–280.

11. Quote from *OR,* ser. 1, vol. 27, pt. 3:134.

12. *OR,* ser. 1, vol. 27, pt. 2:280; Bates, *Pennsylvania Volunteers* 3:1145.

13. Gen. Benjamin Kelley (1807–1891), a native of New Hampshire, organized the First (West) Virginia Infantry. He was wounded at Philippi and later guarded the Baltimore and Ohio Railroad. In 1865 he, along with Gen. George Crooke, was captured by Confederate partisans. Warner, *Generals in Blue,* 260–61.

14. New Creek Station, West Virginia, was on the Baltimore and Ohio Railroad, southeast of Piedmont.

15. Sgt. William J. Stiffler was mustered into service on January 8, 1862, for three years. He was captured at Bunker Hill, Virginia, on January 1, 1864, and died at the Confederate prison camp at Andersonville, Georgia, on May 8, 1864; see John Black's letter of December 28, 1864, for details of Stiffler's death. Bates, *Pennsylvania Volunteers* 3:1166; *Philadelphia Inquirer,* July 2, 1863.

16. While the regiment suffered just 4 killed and 12 wounded, more than 150 men fell captive into Confederate hands. Unfortunately, the published company roster does not indicate the names of Company G's casualties in the battle. Bates, *Pennsylvania Volunteers* 3:1165–68.

17. Black was incorrect in his assertion that the Union Army had outmaneuvered the Confederates and was approaching Richmond. In actuality, Army of the Potomac commander George Meade received much criticism for his slow pursuit of the retreating rebels. See Eicher, *Longest Night,* 552–53.

18. During the summer of 1863, the Federal government resorted to a draft in order to obtain the necessary number of new recruits. There was much opposition to the draft, particularly in New York City. This culminated in the anti-draft riots of July 1863. See James W. Geary, *We Need Men: The Union Draft in the Civil War* (DeKalb: Northern Illinois Univ., 1991).

19. Stephen D. Engle, *Thunder in the Hills: A History of the Civil War in Jefferson County, West Virginia* (Charleston, W.Va.: Mountain State Press, 1989), 43–46, provides a good account of this action. The official reports can be found in *OR,* ser. 1, vol. 29, pt. 1:485–92.

20. The regimental history of the Twelfth Pennsylvania indicates that the new officer who took command at Martinsburg was likely the Twelfth's Lt. Col. William Bell, though he was not actually promoted to lieutenant colonel until the spring of 1864. Col. Lewis B. Pierce was in command of the regiment until his discharge in late 1864. Maier, *Leather and Steel,* 142; Bates, *Pennsylvania Volunteers* 3:1148.

21. Evidently the "Protracted Meeting" mentioned by Black was connected to a religious revival taking place among the men of the Twelfth and perhaps the local population. Black and Jennie were both Methodists.

22. George H. Hammer served as chaplain of the Twelfth Cavalry. He was mustered into service on March 22, 1862, as captain of Company B, and was appointed chaplain on May 15 of the same year. Hammer was discharged on a surgeon's certificate of disability on March 5, 1865. Bates, *Pennsylvania Volunteers* 3:1149.

23. For religion and Civil War soldiers, see Steven E. Woodworth, *While God Is Marching On: The Religious World of Civil War Soldiers* (Lawrence: Univ. Press of Kansas, 2001); and George Rable, *God's Almost Chosen Peoples: A Religious History of the American Civil War* (Chapel Hill: Univ. of North Carolina Press, 2010).

Chapter 4

1. See for example, McPherson, *For Cause and Comrades;* Gerald F. Linderman, *Embattled Courage: The Experience of Combat in the American Civil War* (New York: Free Press, 1987); and Mitchell, *Vacant Chair.* The Union high command eventually disallowed officer resignations at any time.

2. Bates, *Pennsylvania Volunteers* 3:1146

3. See also *OR*, ser. 1, vol. 33, pp. 321–25, 479, 509, 847.

4. William Woods Averell (1832–1900) was a regular army officer who, upon the outbreak of the war, served initially as colonel of the Third Pennsylvania Cavalry and then as commander of the Army of the Potomac's Second Cavalry Division from February to May 1863. Relieved after the Battle of Chancellorsville, Averell then took command of the Fourth Separate Brigade, Eighth Corps, in western Virginia until April 1864 and then again commanded the Second Cavalry Division. After the September 1864 battle of Fisher's Hill, Averell was relieved by General Sheridan for his slow pursuit of the retreating Confederates. Warner, *Generals in Blue*, 12–13.

5. See note 15 in chapter 3, above, for biographical information on Stiffler, whose captors sent him to Andersonville. For the skirmish at Bunker Hill, see Maier, *Leather and Steel*, 144–45.

6. On Belle Isle, see Boatner, *Civil War Dictionary*, 57.

7. Compiled Service Record of John H. Black and Pension File of John H. Black; miscellaneous clippings relating to Black, private collection of Marguerite Campbell; Bates, *Pennsylvania Volunteers* 3:1146; Taylor, *Philadelphia in the Civil War*, 170–71.

8. Joseph F. Lunday/Lundy was mustered into service in Company G on March 28, 1864, and mustered out on July 20, 1865. Bates, *Pennsylvania Volunteers* 3:1167.

9. *OR*, ser. 1, vol. 37, pt. 1:162. Brig. Gen. Max Weber reported that a scouting party from the Twelfth Cavalry was sent into Loudoun County after Mosby's men. The Pennsylvanians "scattered the party, took 8 men prisoners and 7 horses, and returned without any loss."

10. John W. Hicks was mustered into service as captain of Company C, Seventy-sixth Pennsylvania Infantry on October 17, 1861. Subsequently promoted to major and lieutenant colonel, he was wounded at Battery Wagner in July 1863 and mustered out on June 1, 1864, as a result of his wound. Bates, *Pennsylvania Volunteers* 2:949.

11. John Black's brother Samuel appears on the 1850 federal census as a fourteen-year-old schoolboy, living with his parents Jacob and Mary Black and his six siblings in Blair County, Pennsylvania. He does not appear to be living with the family in the 1860 census, though a Samuel Black of about the correct age is listed in Cambria County. He is living in the household of "Ore Miner" Isaac Speer, and his occupation is listed as "Teamster." There are nineteen Samuel Blacks listed as serving in Pennsylvania units during the Civil War. It is not known if one is the "Brother Samuel" to which John Black referred, or if his brother actually served during the war. Hewett, *Roster of Union Soldiers* 1:126; 1850 federal census, Blair County, Pa.; 1860 federal census, Cambria County, Pa.

12. Unidentified. Mollie could perhaps be the Mollie Slayman mentioned in several other of Black's letters.

13. A John Laise was mustered into Company C, Seventy-sixth Pennsylvania Infantry on October 17, 1861, and mustered out on July 18, 1865. Bates, *Pennsylvania Volunteers* 2:960.

14. Joseph E. Engle enlisted as a farrier in Company G on February 29, 1864, to serve for three years. He was mustered out with his company on July 20, 1865. Bates, *Pennsylvania Volunteers* 3:1166.

15. Cpl. John F. Gardner of Company G was mustered into service on February 13, 1862. He was captured by Confederate forces on February 3, 1864, and subsequently released. He was discharged by special order on April 15, 1865. Bates, *Pennsylvania Volunteers* 3:1166.

16. Engle, *Thunder in the Hills;* Maier, *Leather and Steel,* 180–99; Bates, *Pennsylvania Volunteers* 3:1146–48; *OR*, ser. 1, vol. 37, pt. 1:286–331. Good accounts of the Shenandoah campaigns are Jeffry D. Wert, *From Winchester to Cedar Creek: The Shenandoah Campaign of 1864* (Carlisle, Pa.: South Mountain Press, 1987); and Edward J. Stackpole, *Sheridan in the Shenandoah: Jubal Early's Nemesis* (Harrisburg, Pa.: Stackpole Co.,

1861); Paul Magid, *George Crook : From the Redwoods to Appomattox* (Norman: Univ. of Oklahoma Press, 2011), 216–19; see also Scott C. Patchan, *Shenandoah Summer: The 1864 Valley Campaign* (Lincoln: Univ. of Nebraska Press, 2007), 225–26. According to Patchan, "The 12th Pennsylvania Cavalry spearheaded the charge, but the regiment had a poor combat record. Tibbits had only recently warned their commander 'if he did not fight his regiment well, he would open artillery on them.' Lacking cannon at Kernstown, Tibbits resorted to inspiration, calling out, 'The 12th would lick any brigade in the valley,' as the Pennsylvanians surged past. They stormed into Mr. Pritchard's orchard, striking the 60th Virginia of Smith's brigade and 2nd Virginia of Terry's. The initial shock of the charge briefly checked the Virginians and allowed the Federal ambulance train to escape. An admiring Confederate thought Tibbits's charge 'very daring.' Nevertheless, once the Virginians recovered and began firing at the Federal cavalry, the onlooker thought that it looked as though 'every man was killed or captured.' Tibbits's brigade lost heavily in this sacrificial charge, including two officers of the 12th Pennsylvania who fell in the effort."

17. The "great scare" Black mentions is a reference to Confederate general Jubal Early's invasion of Maryland that summer. For an overview of the campaign, see Frank Vandiver, *Jubal's Raid: General Early's Famous Attack on Washington in 1864* (New York: McGraw-Hill, 1960).

18. Maier, *Leather and Steel,* 199–200, believes that Black may be describing "the Union attempt to repulse the . . . crossing of the Potomac River at Shepherdstown, West Virginia by Confederate cavalry," but he adds, "Why he would describe the engagement as a victory, when in fact the Federals were brushed away from the Antietam Ford, is a mystery."

19. There are a number of individuals with the surname Black living in Indiana County in the 1860 census, but none with the first name of Maggie or Margaret. 1860 federal census, Indiana County, Pa.

20. Black's surviving correspondence gives no further indication as to the identity of the "folks at the Toll gate." Likewise, the details of Black's "scratch" on July 4 are not elaborated on further. On that day, elements of Jubal Early's Confederate force threatened Harpers Ferry as they passed through the area before moving eastward toward Washington, D.C. Lt. Col. William Bell commanded the troopers of the Twelfth Pennsylvania guarding the Union lines on Bolivar Heights. Bell's men, including evidently John Black, "fought a sharp, though probably brief delaying action" before being driven from their position. Bell was later criticized by at least two fellow officers of the Twelfth for incompetence in failing to provide his men with sufficient ammunition before the engagement. Maier, *Leather and Steel,* 185–88; Vandiver, *Jubal's Raid,* 82–88; *OR,* ser. 1, vol. 37, pt. 2:41.

21. Engle, *Thunder in the Hills,* 59–65; Maier, *Leather and Steel,* 204–7; *OR,* ser. 1, vol. 43, pt. 1:424–25, 874–75.

22. William Bell was mustered into service on March 21, 1862, as a captain of Company F, to serve for three years. He was promoted to major on April 25, 1862, and to lieutenant colonel on July 2, 1864. He was discharged by special order on October 5, 1864. Bates, *Pennsylvania Volunteers* 3:1163.

23. It is unclear which adjutant Black is mentioning, perhaps Graves B. Hammer. See Bates, *Pennsylvania Volunteers* 3:1149 for a list of all adjutants in the Twelfth Cavalry.

24. The battle that Black is referring to is the Battle of Cameron's Depot. Engle, *Thunder in the Hills,* 59–65; Maier, *Leather and Steel,* 204–7; *OR,* ser. 1, vol. 43, pt. 1:424–25, 874–75.

25. During the summer and fall of 1864, Union major general Philip Sheridan operated in the Shenandoah Valley against Confederate forces under Gen. Jubal Early. The result was a series of smashing victories for the Federals, including the Third Battle of Winchester (or the Battle of Opequon Creek), fought September 19, in which Sheridan drove Early out of Winchester in retreat farther south in the Shenandoah Valley. The Battle of Fisher's Hill was also a Union victory fought near the town of Strasburg, Virginia, on September 21–22, in which Sheridan's army forced Early's army to retreat to Waynesboro. Although defeated, Early's Confederates were not destroyed and would subsequently attempt to regain the initiative when Early attacked the Federals at Cedar Creek on October 19. The cumulative effect of these battles, however, was that they largely cleared the Shenandoah of regular Confederate troops for the remainder of the war. See Gary W. Gallagher, *The Shenandoah Valley Campaign of 1864* (Chapel Hill: Univ. of North Carolina Press, 2006); see also Patchan, *Shenandoah Summer;* and Boatner, *Civil War Dictionary,* 743–46.

26. In early 1864, Lt. Gen. Ulysses S. Grant was appointed general in chief of the Union armies. George Meade remained in command of the Army of the Potomac, and Grant maintained his headquarters with Meade's force. Warner, *Generals in Blue,* 183–86, 315–17.

27. Engle, *Thunder in the Hills,* 68–70; Festus D. Summers, *The Baltimore and Ohio in the Civil War* (New York: G. P. Putnam's Sons, 1939), 174–75; Virgil Carrington Jones, *Ranger Mosby* (Chapel Hill: Univ. of North Carolina Press, 1944), 216–20; *OR,* ser. 1, vol. 43, pt. 2:368–72. See also James Ramage, *Gray Ghost: The Life of Col. John Singleton Mosby* (Lexington: Univ. Press of Kentucky, 1999), 228–70; and Jeffry Wert, *Mosby's Rangers* (New York: Simon and Schuster, 1991), 231–36.

28. *OR,* ser. 1, vol. 43, pt. 2:391.

29. Ibid., 665.

30. See David E. Long, *The Jewel of Liberty: Abraham Lincoln and the End of Slavery* (Mechanicsburg, Pa.: Stackpole, 1994), 215–34; John C. Waugh, *Reelecting Lincoln: The Battle for the 1864 Presidency* (New York: Crown, 1997); Oscar O. Winther, "The Soldier Vote in the Election of 1864," *New York History* 25 (Oct. 1944): 440–58; T. Harry Williams, "Voters in Blue: The Citizen Soldiers of the Civil War," *Mississippi Valley Historical Review* 31 (Sept. 1944): 187–204; Maier, *Leather and Steel*, 246–47.

31. John H. Black Letter (Ms 1989-089), Special Collections, University Libraries, Virginia Polytechnic Institute and State University, Blacksburg, Virginia.

32. The victory Black refers to was at Cedar Creek on October 19. In the engagement, Jubal Early's Confederate force attacked and routed a portion of Philip Sheridan's Union army before the Northern commander, returning to his troops following a meeting in Washington, rallied his men and directed the counterattack that drove the Confederates from the field. The fight left the Shenandoah in the hands of the Federals. See Stackpole, *Sheridan in the Shenandoah*, 281–365, and Wert, From *Winchester to Cedar Creek*, 169–238.

33. *OR*, ser. 1, vol. 43, pt. 2, p. 798.

34. *OR*, ser. 1, vol. 46, p. 455; see also Stephen Starr, *The Union Cavalry in the Civil War*, 3 vols. (Baton Rouge: Louisiana State Univ. Press, 1979–85), vol. 2:342–49, 361–64.

35. Unidentified. Perhaps a relative of Jennie's. There are numerous men named John Walter or John Walters who served in Pennsylvania units, including five from Blair County alone. Hewett, *Roster of Union Soldiers* 4:166–68; Hoenstine, *Military Services and Genealogical Records*, 272.

36. During the Civil War, the Corps of Engineers performed duties such as the construction of defensive fortifications, as well as bridges, roads, and other facilities. While some engineer regiments were established, it is likely that Evans was on temporary duty with a group performing engineer functions. Terry L. Jones, *The A to Z of the Civil War*, 2 vols. (Lanham, Md.: Scarecrow Press, 2006), vol. 1:461.

37. The *Guidon* was a camp newspaper published irregularly by the Twelfth Cavalry during late 1864 and early 1865. At least one issue, volume 1, no. 4, December 22, 1864, is known to survive at the American Antiquarian Society in Worcester, Massachusetts. The St. Louis Historical Society in St. Louis, Missouri, also has nine issues from November 26, 1864, to February 10, 1865.

38. Pvt. Elias Bowen of Company E was the victim. He was mustered into service on October 4, 1864, for one year and died at Charles Town on December 25, 1864. The murderer was James Montgomery, who is listed as absent in arrest at the mustering out of the regiment. His name does not appear in a compiled list of Union soldiers executed during the war. Bates,

Pennsylvania Volunteers 3:1161–62. Additional details of the incident can be found in Maier, *Leather and Steel*, 252–53; and Robert J. Alotta, *Civil War Justice: Union Army Executions Under Lincoln* (Shippensburg, Pa.: White Mane, 1989), 202–9.

39. The December 29, 1864, issue of the *Guidon* includes an obituary for Sgt. William J. Stiffler, which was written by Black and signed "B." It states, "Sergt. Stiffler was one of the first to answer the call of the President for men to suppress the rebellion. . . . He served faithfully and bravely with his company until July 24, 1863, when in a skirmish at McConnelsburg, PA., he was wounded in the left shoulder." Stiffler was then captured on January 1, 1864, near Bunker Hill, Virginia. Following his capture, he "suffer[ed] for four months and eight days under the cruel and barbarous treatment of southern chivalry, death alone released him from his misery. In him the country has lost as brave a soldier as ever met the enemy on the field of battle. He was beloved by all who knew him." Stiffler died on May 8, 1864, at the Confederate prison camp at Andersonville.

Chapter 5

1. Bates, *Pennsylvania Volunteers* 3:1148. See James J. Williamson, *Mosby's Rangers: A Record of the Operations of the Forty-third Battalion Virginia Cavalry* (New York: Ralph Kenyon, 1896); John Scott, *Partisan Life with Colonel Mosby* (New York: Harper and Brothers, 1867); and John Munson, *Reminiscences of a Mosby Guerrilla* (1906; reprint, Washington, D.C.: Zenger 1983) for details on Mosby's operations. See also Wert, *Mosby's Rangers*, 259–86; Ramage, *Gray Ghost*. See Hearns, *Six Years of Hell*, 231–86, for military operations in the vicinity, 1864–65.

2. Courts-martial adjudicated cases arising out of alleged offenses of military regulations. According to army regulations, "General courts-martial may consist of any number of commissioned officers, from five to thirteen, inclusively; but they shall not consist of less than thirteen where that number can be convened without manifest injury to the service." Other types of courts-martial might consist of a smaller number of officers. Regimental and corps commanders, as well as the commanders of "garrisons, forts, barracks, or other places where the troops consist of different corps," could appoint courts-martial consisting of three officers. U.S. War Department, *The 1863 Laws of War, Articles of War, General Orders 100, General Orders 49, Extracts of Revised Army Regulations of 1861* (reprint, Mechanicsburg, Pa.: Stackpole, 2005), 17–27.

3. Black's meaning is unclear, given the fact that both he and Jennie were Methodists. Perhaps he simply meant that he and Jennie could not fully practice their religious beliefs until he had left the army and they were together.

4. Marcus Albert Reno (1835–1889) graduated from West Point in 1857, twentieth in a class of thirty-eight. He initially served in the First Dragoons and the First Cavalry, before being appointed colonel of the Twelfth Cavalry in January 1865. Following the Civil War, Reno taught tactics at West Point and was head of the New Orleans Freedmen's Bureau. He later was assigned to the Seventh United States Cavalry, a portion of which he commanded during George Armstrong Custer's disastrous 1876 campaign. Accused of cowardice during that battle, Reno turned increasingly to drink and was dismissed from the army in 1880. For the best account of Reno's life and military career, see Ronald H. Nichols, *In Custer's Shadow: Major Marcus Reno* (Norman: Univ. of Oklahoma Press, 1999), 65–75.

5. Moses K. Garland mustered into Company C, Seventy-sixth Pennsylvania Infantry on March 28, 1864, and was killed in action at Chapin's Farm (Chaffin's Farm), Virginia, on January 1, 1865. Bates, *Pennsylvania Volunteers* 2:960.

6. David M. Ginter mustered into Company G on January 8, 1862. He was promoted from quartermaster sergeant to first sergeant on February 7, 1865, and was mustered out on July 20, 1865. Bates, *Pennsylvania Volunteers* 3:1166.

7. John Brissell was mustered into Company G on February 27, 1864, and discharged by general order on June 15, 1865. Bates, *Pennsylvania Volunteers* 3:1166.

8. Among the men sentenced to death were Luther T. Palmer and William Randall of the Fifth New York Artillery; James Lynch, alias Hennessy, of the Second New York Cavalry; James Brown, unit unknown; and men with the last names of Jackson and Stewart, units also unknown. Luther and Lynch were sentenced for desertion, while the crimes of the others are unknown. Basler, *Collected Works of Abraham Lincoln* 8:297–98, 300–301.

9. Pvt. John Frye/Fry was mustered into service for three years on February 22, 1864. He was killed at Charles Town, West Virginia, on February 7, 1865. Bates, *Pennsylvania Volunteers* 3:1167.

10. David A. Gildae had served with Black in 1861 in the Fourteenth Pennsylvania Infantry. He was mustered in as first sergeant for three months' service in April 1861. Bates, *Pennsylvania Volunteers* 1:140.

11. Black was promoted to first lieutenant on February 6, 1865. Compiled Service Record of John H. Black.

12. Unidentified.

13. Andrew McGough was mustered into Company G on January 18, 1862, for three years. He was promoted to first sergeant and subsequently to second lieutenant, on April 29, 1864, and was mustered out with his company on July 20, 1865. Bates, *Pennsylvania Volunteers* 3:1166.

14. On February 17, President Lincoln wired the "officer in command at Harpers Ferry" that he should "suspend [the] execution of sentence" in the cases of Jackson, Stewart, and Randall "until further orders and forward records of trials for examination." That same day, Brig. Gen. John Stevenson reported that "the order suspending the execution of Jackson[,] Stewart & Randall has been duly obeyed." Lincoln had previously ordered suspension of the death sentences for Brown, Lynch, Palmer, and Randall. Basler, *Collected Works of Abraham Lincoln* 8:297–98, 300–301.

15. There are numerous Charles Gardners listed as serving in Pennsylvania units, but Black is likely referring to the individual from Blair County who served in the First Pennsylvania Cavalry. Gardner was mustered in on October 20, 1862, for three years' service. After serving as a private in Company G he became a hospital steward in the same regiment. Hewett, *Roster of Union Soldiers* 2:40; Bates, *Pennsylvania Volunteers* 1:1026.

16. The regimental history of the Twelfth Pennsylvania provides no additional information as to the issue of furloughs, or to why certain individuals received them and others did not. By March 1865, however, it was clear that the period of active campaigning was close to beginning, and guerrilla activity in the lower Shenandoah had picked up in recent months. Colonel Reno, however, was on a twenty-day furlough as late as mid-March, though his leave would be cut short and he would be called back to the regiment early. Maier, *Leather and Steel,* 278–93.

17. This rumor proved false in that Sheridan did not capture Early but defeated the last major remnant of Early's forces in the Shenandoah at Waynesboro on March 2, 1865. Sheridan then moved against Charlottesville, with George Custer's cavalry in the vanguard, which he occupied the following day. Ervin L. Jordan Jr., *Charlottesville and the University of Virginia in the Civil War* (Lynchburg, Va.: H. E. Howard, 1989), 82–84.

18. James P. Stewart enlisted in Company G on August 2, 1862, and was discharged by general order on June 1, 1865. Bates, *Pennsylvania Volunteers* 3:1166.

19. James E. McHugh was mustered into service on March 30, 1864, for three years. He was killed in action near Charles Town on March 13, 1865, when a four-man patrol from the Twelfth was ambushed by Confederates. Bates, *Pennsylvania Volunteers* 3:1167; Maier, *Leather and Steel,* 292.

20. In addition to the death of McHugh, Sgt. Frank McKusker and Pvt. Thomas Wagner were captured, while Pvt. John A. Pitcho was badly wounded but reached Union lines. Maier, *Leather and Steel,* 292.

21. *OR*, ser. 1, vol. 46, pt. 1:535–36.

22. Ibid.

23. Briscoe Goodhart, *History of the Independent Loudoun Virginia Rangers, U.S. Vol. Cav. (Scouts), 1862–1865* (Washington, D.C.: Press of McGill and Wallace, 1896), 191–92; J. G. Wiltshire, " Mosby's Men," *Confederate Veteran* 8, no. 2 (1896): 74–75.

24. Maier, *Leather and Steel*, 299. Pages 293–301 of Maier's work cover the entire expedition.

25. "On the Scout," *National Tribune*, Dec. 15, 1898.

26. Ibid. "Pantaloons" quote from John Black letter of May 9, 1865.

27. The telegram was with the Black correspondence until the 1980s, but it unfortunately is now separated from the remainder of the material.

28. *Altoona Mirror*, Apr. 11, 1908.

29. Ibid.; also Compiled Service Record of John H. Black and Pension File of John H. Black. Bates, *Pennsylvania Volunteers* 3:1148, provides an outline of the unit's last months of service. During the course of the war the regiment suffered 34 soldiers killed in action and 108 dead of disease. Dyer, *Compendium* 2:1564.

30. The following letter was written by relatives of Jennie after they had heard news of John Black's wounding.

31. William A. Leighty was born in Duncansville, Blair County, Pennsylvania, on May 20, 1827. In 1860 he lived in Blair County with his wife Mary and their three children, Clara, Millard, and Ann. Ten years later he and Mary resided in Ebensburg, Pennsylvania, with six children. He listed his occupation as a wagon maker. He died in Ebensburg on June 6, 1892. 1860 federal census, Blair County, Pa.; 1870 federal census, Cambria County, Pa.

32. John Dunlap Stevenson (1821–1897) was a native of Staunton, Virginia. He organized a Missouri unit that fought in the Mexican War and served in the state legislature. He fought in the Western theater from 1862 to 1864 before resigning his commission in April of the latter year. In August 1864 he was reappointed a brigadier general and placed in command of the District of Harpers Ferry. He served in this capacity until the end of the war. Warner, *Generals in Blue*, 476–77.

33. Capt. James W. Grubb served initially as commander of Company B of the Independent Loudoun, Virginia Rangers, U.S. Volunteer Cavalry, and later as commander of the entire battalion. This unit, originally organized in 1862 as a separate company and eventually expanded into a battalion, was composed of Virginia unionists. It proved very successful in conducting counter-insurgency operations against Confederate partisans.

34. Unidentified. The 1860 census returns include the name of a William A. Gore, who lived in or near Winchester. He was a thirty-eight-year-old native of Virginia. 1860 federal census, Frederick County, Va.

35. Pvt. Jno. H. Williamson was mustered into service for three years on February 13, 1862. He was mustered out with his company on July 20, 1865. Bates, *Pennsylvania Volunteers* 3:1168.

36. E. P. Hostetter, mustered in March 1, 1862, and mustered out July 20, 1865. Bates, *Pennsylvania Volunteers* 3:1152.

37. W. H. McAllister was promoted from captain to lieutenant colonel on May 18, 1865, and was mustered out on July 20, 1865. Bates, *Pennsylvania Volunteers* 3:1148.

38. John Johnson was promoted from captain to major on May 3, 1865, and was mustered out on July 20, 1865. Bates, *Pennsylvania Volunteers* 3:1149.

39. Thomas Ivory was mustered into service in Company G on January 8, 1862, and died at the Confederate prison camp at Salisbury, North Carolina, on January 15, 1865. Bates, *Pennsylvania Volunteers* 3:1167.

40. Christian Speece was mustered into service on February 25, 1864, and captured on June 29, 1864. He was discharged by general order on June 15, 1865. Bates, *Pennsylvania Volunteers* 3:1162.

41. Benjamin F. Stewart was mustered into service in Company G on September 20, 1864, and discharged by general order on May 26, 1865. Bates, *Pennsylvania Volunteers* 3:1167.

42. Louis Fetters was mustered into service on February 29, 1864, and discharged by general order on May 17, 1865. Bates, *Pennsylvania Volunteers* 3:1166.

43. Conrad Fleck was mustered into service on February 29, 1864, and discharged by general order on May 26, 1865. Bates, *Pennsylvania Volunteers* 3:1166.

44. Aaron Daugherty was mustered in on January 8, 1862. He was promoted from sergeant to quartermaster sergeant on February 7, 1865, and was mustered out on July 20, 1865. Bates, *Pennsylvania Volunteers* 3:1166.

45. War Department General Orders No. 86, dated May 9, 1865, called for boards to examine "the relative merit of the officers of their regiments or departments" and to determine "what officers, in the opinion of the boards, should be discharged." *OR*, ser. 3, vol. 5, p. 15. The writer is incorrect in that the Twelfth Pennsylvania was not consolidated with any other units. It remained a separate regiment until it was mustered out in late July 1865. The unit's regimental history makes no mention of boards of examination for surplus officers actually taking place, but since the consolidation did not occur, the examinations may have been unnecessary. See Maier, *Leather and Steel,* 304–13 for details on the regiment's activities in the period prior to its mustering out.

46. Col. Marcus Albert Reno received a brevet promotion to brigadier general, United States Volunteers, on March 13, 1865, for "meritorious services

during the war." Roger D. Hunt and Jack R. Brown, *Brevet Brigadier Generals in Blue* (Gaithersburg, Md.: Olde Soldier Books, 1990), 502.

47. William J. Blackwood was mustered into service in Company G on January 24, 1862. He was discharged on February 17, 1865, on the expiration of his term. Bates, *Pennsylvania Volunteers* 3:1166.

Chapter 6

1. John H. Black obituary; Sell, *Twentieth Century History,* 657–58; 1850, 1860, 1870, 1880, 1900, and 1910 federal censuses, Blair County, Pa.

2. John H. Black obituary. Black was never promoted to captain, finishing his army career as first lieutenant. In later years, however, he was often referred to by the honorary rank of captain.

3. Pension File of John H. Black.

4. Ibid.

5. Ibid.

6. *Altoona Mirror,* Apr. 4, 1908.

7. Pension File of John H. Black.

8. Ibid.; John H. Black obituary.

Bibliography

Manuscripts

Black, John H. Clippings and photographs. Private collection of Marguerite Campbell. Claysburg, Pa.

Black, John H. Collection. Photocopies. Private collection of David Coles. Farmville, Va.

Black, John H. Letter. MS 1989-089. Special Collections, University Libraries, Virginia Polytechnic Institute and State University.

Black, John H., and the Twelfth Pennsylvania Cavalry. Miscellaneous papers. Blair County Genealogical Society, Hollidaysburg, Pa.

Congdon, James A. Letters, 1862–65. Collection 1620. Historical Society of Pennsylvania, Philadelphia.

Twelfth Pennsylvania Cavalry. Miscellaneous papers. Civil War Library and Museum, Philadelphia.

National Archives and Record Administration. Washington, D.C.

   Compiled Service Record of John H. Black.

   Federal census records for Pennsylvania, 1850–1920.

   Federal census records for Virginia, 1860.

   Pension File of John H. Black.

   Loose and bound records of the Twelfth Pennsylvania Cavalry.

Records of the Middle Military Division.

Weirick, Charles. Papers. United States Army Military History Institute. Carlisle, Pa.

Newspapers and Periodicals

Altoona (Pa.) Mirror.

Confederate Veteran.

Guidon.

National Tribune (Washington, D.C.).

Philadelphia Inquirer.

Southern Historical Society Papers.

Books

Africa, J. Simpson. *History of Huntingdon and Blair Counties, Pennsylvania.* N.p., n.d.

Alotta, Robert J. *Civil War Justice: Union Army Executions Under Lincoln.* Shippensburg, Pa.: White Mane, 1989.

Basler, Roy P. *The Collected Works of Abraham Lincoln.* 8 vols. New Brunswick, N.J.: Rutgers Univ. Press, 1953.

Bates, Samuel P. *Pennsylvania Volunteers, 1861–1865.* 5 vols. Harrisburg, Pa.: B. Singerly, 1869–71.

Beach, William H. *The First New York (Lincoln) Cavalry.* N.p.: Lincoln Cavalry Association, 1902.

Blair, William, and William Pencak, eds. *Making and Remaking Pennsylvania's Civil War.* University Park: Pennsylvania State Univ. Press, 2001.

Boatner, Mark, III. *The Civil War Dictionary.* New York: David McKay, 1959.

Bonnell, John C., Jr. *Sabres in the Shenandoah: The 21st New York Cavalry, 1863–1866.* Shippensburg, Pa.: Burd Street Press, 1996.

Bushong, Millard K. *Historic Jefferson County.* Boyce, Va.: Carr, 1972.

Coddington, Edwin B. *The Gettysburg Campaign: A Study in Command.* New York: Charles Scribner's Sons, 1968.

Cohen, Stan. *The Civil War in West Virginia: A Pictorial History.* Charleston, W.Va.: Pictorial Histories, 1981.

Costa, Dora L., and Matthew E. Kahn. *Heroes and Cowards: The Social Face of War.* Princeton, N.J.: Princeton Univ. Press, 2008.

Delauter, Roger U., Jr. *Winchester in the Civil War.* Lynchburg, Va.: H. E. Howard, 1992.

Drickamer, Lee C., and Karen D. Drickamer. *Fort Lyon to Harpers Ferry: On the Border of North and South with "Rambling Jour."* Shippensburg, Pa.: White Mane, 1987.

Dunaway, Wayland Fuller. *A History of Pennsylvania.* New York: Prentice-Hall, 1935.

Duncan, Richard R. *Beleaguered Winchester: A Virginia Community at War, 1861–1865.* Baton Rouge: Louisiana State Univ. Press, 2007.

———. *Lee's Endangered Left: The Civil War in West Virginia.* Baton Rouge: Louisiana State Univ. Press, 2004.

Dyer, Frederick H. *A Compendium of the War of the Rebellion.* 2 vols. 1908. Reprint, Dayton, Ohio: Press of Morningside Bookshop, 1978.

Eby, Cecil D., Jr., ed. *A Virginia Yankee in the Civil War: The Diaries of David Hunter Strother.* Chapel Hill: Univ. of North Carolina Press, 1961.

Eicher, David J. *The Longest Night: A Military History of the Civil War.* New York: Simon & Schuster, 2001.

Engle, Stephen Douglas. *Thunder in the Hills: A History of Jefferson County, West Virginia During the American Civil War.* Charleston, W.Va.: Mountain State Press, 1989.

Faust, Drew G. *This Republic of Suffering: Death and the American Civil War.* New York: Alfred Knopf, 2008.

Faust, Patricia, ed. *Historical Times Illustrated Encyclopedia of the Civil War.* New York: Harper & Row, 1986.

Fellman, Michael. *Inside War: The Guerrilla Conflict in Missouri During the American Civil War.* New York: Oxford Univ. Press, 1989.

Furgurson, Ernest B. *Freedom Rising: Washington in the Civil War.* New York: Alfred A. Knopf, 2004.

Gallagher, Gary W. *The Shenandoah Valley Campaign of 1864.* Chapel Hill: Univ. of North Carolina Press, 2006.

Geary James W. *We Need Men: The Union Draft in the Civil War.* DeKalb: Northern Illinois Univ. Press, 1991.

Gilmor, Harry. *Four Years in the Saddle.* New York: Harper & Row, 1866.

Goodhart, Briscoe. *History of the Independent Loudoun Virginia Rangers, U.S. Vol. Cav. (Scouts), 1862–1865.* Washington, D.C.: Press of McGill and Wallace, 1896.

Grunder, Charles S., and Brandon H. Beck. *The Second Battle of Winchester, June 12–15, 1863.* Lynchburg, Va.: H. E. Howard, 1989.

Hearn, Chester G. *Six Years of Hell: Harpers Ferry During the Civil War.* Baton Rouge: Louisiana State Univ. Press, 1996.

Heidler, David S., and Jeanne T. Heidler, eds. *Encyclopedia of the American Civil War: A Political, Social, and Military History.* 5 vols. Santa Barbara, Calif.: ABC-Clio, 2000.

Hennessy, John J. *Return to Bull Run: The Campaign and Battle of Second Manassas.* New York: Simon & Schuster, 1993.

Hesseltine, William B. *Lincoln and the War Governors.* New York: Alfred A. Knopf, 1948.

Hewett, Janet B., ed. *Roster of Union Soldiers, 1861–1865.* 33 vols. Wilmington, N.C.: Broadfoot, 1997–2001.

———. *Supplement to the Official Records of the Union and Confederate Armies.* 100 vols. Wilmington, N.C.: Broadfoot, 1994–2001.

Hoenstine, Floyd G. *Military Services and Genealogical Records of Soldiers of Blair County, Pennsylvania.* Hollidaysburg, Pa.: n.p., 1940.

Hunt, Roger D., and Jack R. Brown. *Brevet Brigadier Generals in Blue.* Gaithersburg, Md.: Olde Soldier Books, 1990.

Jimerson, Randall. *The Private Civil War: Popular Thought During the Sectional Conflict.* Baton Rouge: Louisiana State Univ. Press, 1988.

Jones, Terry L. *The A to Z of the Civil War.* 2 vols. Lanham, Md.: Scarecrow Press, 2006.

Jones, Virgil Carrington. *Gray Ghosts and Rebel Raiders.* New York: Holt, 1956.

———. *Ranger Mosby.* Chapel Hill: Univ. of North Carolina Press, 1944.

Jordan, Ervin L., Jr. *Charlottesville and the University of Virginia in the Civil War.* Lynchburg, Va.: H. E. Howard, 1989.

Keen, Hugh C., and Horace Mewborn. *43rd Battalion Virginia Cavalry Mosby's Command.* Lynchburg, Va.: H. E. Howard, 1993.

Kellog, Sanford Cobb. *The Shenandoah Valley and Virginia 1861 to 1865.* New York: Neale, 1903.

Leech, Margaret. *Reveille in Washington, 1860–1865.* New York: Harper and Brothers, 1941.

Linderman, Gerald F. *Embattled Courage: The Experience of Combat in the American Civil War.* New York: Free Press, 1987.

Long, David E. *The Jewel of Liberty: Abraham Lincoln and the End of Slavery.* Mechanicsburg, Pa.: Stackpole, 1994.

Long, E. B. *The Civil War Day by Day: An Almanac, 1861–65.* New York: Doubleday, 1971.

Lord, Francis A. *Civil War Sutlers and Their Wares.* New York: T. Yoseloff, 1969.

Lystra, Karen. *Searching the Heart: Women, Men, and Romantic Love in Nineteenth-Century America.* New York: Oxford Univ. Press, 1989.

Mackey, Robert. *The Uncivil War: Irregular Warfare in the Upper South, 1861–1865.* Norman: Univ. of Oklahoma Press, 2004.

Maier, Larry B. *Gateway to Gettysburg: The Second Battle of Winchester.* Shippensburg, Pa.: White Mane, 2002.

———. *Leather and Steel: The 12th Pennsylvania Cavalry in the Civil War.* Shippensburg, Pa.: Burd Street Press, 2001.

McPherson, James M. *Battle Cry of Freedom: The Civil War Era.* New York: Oxford Univ. Press, 1988.

———. *For Cause and Comrades: Why Men Fought in the Civil War.* New York: Oxford Univ. Press, 1997.

Mewborn, Horace, comp. *"From Mosby's Command": Newspaper Letters and Articles by and about John S. Mosby and His Rangers.* Baltimore: Butternut and Blue, 2005.

Miers, Earl Schenck. *Lincoln Day by Day: A Chronology, 1809–1865.* 3 vols. in 1. Dayton, Ohio: Morningside House, 1991.

Military Operations in Jefferson County, Virginia and West Virginia, 1861–1865. Published by Authority of Jefferson County Camp UCV. 1911. Reprint, n.p.: Whitney and White, 1960.

Miller, Randall M., and William Pencak, eds. *Pennsylvania: A History of the Commonwealth.* University Park: Pennsylvania State Univ. Press, 2002.

Mitchell, Reid. *Civil War Soldiers: Their Expectations and Their Experiences.* New York: Viking Penguin, 1988.

———. *The Vacant Chair: The Northern Soldier Leaves Home.* New York: Oxford Univ. Press, 1993.

Morris, Roy, Jr. *Sheridan: The Life and Wars of General Phil Sheridan.* New York: Crown, 1992.

Mosby, John S. *The Memoirs of Colonel John S. Mosby.* 1917. Reprint, Bloomington: Indiana Univ. Press, 1959.

Munson, John. *Reminiscences of a Mosby Guerrilla.* 1906. Reprint, Washington, D.C.: Zenger, 1983.

Nichols, Ronald H. *In Custer's Shadow: Major Marcus Reno.* Norman: Univ. of Oklahoma Press, 1999.

Nye, Wilbur. *Here Come the Rebels.* Baton Rouge: Louisiana State Univ. Press, 1965.

Oxford English Dictionary. 2nd ed. 1989. http://dictionary.oed.com/.

Patchan, Scott C. *Shenandoah Summer: The 1864 Valley Campaign.* Lincoln: Univ. of Nebraska Press, 2007.

Phillips, Edward H. *The Lower Shenandoah Valley in the Civil War: The Impact of War Upon the Civilian Population and Upon Civil Institutions.* Lynchburg, Va.: H. E. Howard, 1993.

Pinsker, Matthew. *Lincoln's Sanctuary: Abraham Lincoln and the Soldier's Home.* New York: Oxford Univ. Press, 2005.

Pond, George E. *The Shenandoah Valley in 1864.* New York: Charles Scribner's Sons, 1884.

Rable, George. *God's Almost Chosen Peoples: A Religious History of the American Civil War*. Chapel Hill: Univ. of North Carolina Press, 2010.

Ramage, James. *Gray Ghost: The Life of Col. John Singleton Mosby*. Lexington: Univ. Press of Kentucky, 1999.

Regimental Committee. *History of the One Hundred and Twenty-fifth Regiment Pennsylvania Volunteers, 1862–1863*. Philadelphia: J. B. Lippincott, 1906.

Rotundo, E. Anthony. *American Manhood: Transformations in Masculinity from the Revolution to the Modern Era*. New York: Harper Collins, 1993.

Sanders, Charles W. *While in the Hands of the Enemy: Military Prisons of the Civil War*. Baton Rouge: Louisiana State Univ. Press, 2005.

Schroeder-Lein, Glenna, ed. *The Encyclopedia of Civil War Medicine*. Armonk, N.Y.: M. E. Sharpe, 2008.

Scott, John. *Partisan Life with Colonel Mosby*. New York: Harper and Brothers, 1867.

Sell, Jesse C. *Twentieth Century History of Altoona and Blair County, Pennsylvania and Representative Citizens*. Chicago: Richmond-Arnold, 1911.

Smith, Larry D. *150th Anniversary History of Blair County, Pennsylvania*. Apollo, Pa.: Closson Press, 1997.

Stackpole, Edward J. *From Cedar Mountain to Antietam*. Harrisburg, Pa.: Stackpole, 1959.

———. *Sheridan in the Shenandoah: Jubal Early's Nemesis*. Harrisburg, Pa.: Stackpole, 1961.

Starr, Stephen. *The Union Cavalry in the Civil War*. 3 vols. Baton Rouge: Louisiana State Univ. Press, 1979–85.

Summers, Festus P. *The Baltimore and the Ohio in the Civil War*. New York: G. P. Putnam's Sons, 1939.

Sutherland, Daniel E. *A Savage Conflict: The Decisive Role of Guerrillas in the American Civil War*. Chapel Hill: Univ. of North Carolina Press, 2009.

Taylor, Frank H. *Philadelphia in the Civil War, 1861–1865*. Philadelphia: Published by the City, 1913.

Terrell, John Upton. *Faint the Trumpet Sounds: The Life and Trial of Major Reno*. New York: D. McKay, 1966.

U.S. War Department. *The 1863 Laws of War: Articles of War, General Orders 100, General Orders 49 and Extracts of Revised Army Regulations of 1861*. Reprint, Mechanicsburg, Pa.: Stackpole, 2005.

———. *War of the Rebellion: A Compilation of the Official Records of the Union and Confederate Armies*. 128 vols. Washington, D.C.: Government Printing Office, 1880–1901.

Vandiver, Frank. *Jubal's Raid: General Early's Famous Attack on Washington in 1864.* New York: McGraw-Hill, 1960.

Warner, Ezra J. *Generals in Blue: Lives of the Union Commanders.* Baton Rouge: Louisiana State Univ. Press, 1964.

————. *Generals in Gray: Lives of the Confederate Commanders.* Baton Rouge: Louisiana State Univ. Press, 1959.

Waugh, John C. *Reelecting Lincoln: The Battle for the 1864 Presidency.* New York: Crown, 1997.

Wert, Jeffry D. *From Winchester to Cedar Creek: The Shenandoah Campaign of 1864.* Carlisle, Pa.: Stone Mountain Press, 1987.

————. *Mosby's Rangers.* New York: Simon & Schuster, 1990.

Williams, T. Harry. "Voters in Blue: The Citizen Soldiers of the Civil War." *Mississippi Valley Historical Review* 31 (Sept. 1944): 187–204.

Williamson, James J. *Mosby's Rangers: A Record of the Operations of the Forty-third Battalion Virginia Cavalry.* New York: Ralph Kenyon, 1896.

Winther, Oscar O. "The Soldier Vote in the Election of 1864." *New York History* 25 (Oct. 1944): 440–58.

Woodworth, Steven E. *While God Is Marching On: The Religious World of the Civil War Soldier.* Lawrence: Univ. Press of Kansas, 2001.

Index

When the form of a name in the text differs from that in the endnotes, the noted form is used as the main entry and variations found in the text are in parentheses.

A Yankee Horseman in the Shenandoah Valley was designed and typeset on a Macintosh OS 10.4 computer system using InDesign software. The body text is set in 10/13 Sabon and display type is set in Sabon Bold Oldstyle. This book was designed and typeset by Stephanie Thompson and manufactured by Thomson-Shore, Inc.